Evangelization and Christian Development

A book for church workers

Akinbowale Isaac Adewumi

To order additional copies of this book, contact:
Xlibris
1-888-795-4274
www.Xlibris.com
Orders@Xlibris.com
806547

TABLE OF CONTENTS

DEDICATION

*"And say to Archippus, take heed to the
ministry which thou hast received in the
Lord, that thou fulfil it"* – *Colossians 4:17*

To the faithful co-labourers in the Kingdom of God.

PREFACE

E vangelization of the whole world is the greatest concern of our Lord Jesus Christ *"who will have all men to be saved and come to the knowledge of the truth...And he said unto them, Go ye into all the world and preach the gospel to every creature"* (1 Timothy 2:4; Mark 16:15). In this Great Commission, great responsibilities lay on the heads of all believers in Christ to preach the gospel to every creature. It must be understood that every Christian is a soulwinner; but church leaders have matched responsibilities of winning souls and mobilizing and training other believers to win souls for the Lord, regardless of sex, colour or race.

The word "Evangelism" comes from the Greek word "Euaggelion" which means "Gospel" or "Good news" (https://carm.org/what-is-evangelism) of the Kingdom of God and salvation through our Lord Jesus Christ. This message of the gospel includes warning people about sins and its consequences, and the gift of eternal life through genuine repentance and acceptance of Jesus as Lord and Saviour.

This commandment of the Lord is still active, compelling and binding on His Church to obey today, irrespective of geographical locations on the surface of the earth. This is to say that human beings do not live in isolation. There's rather a great deal of interactions among individuals; as such, each individual is identified with a social group which consequently gives him identity. This group is called "a people."

In evangelism, there's need to identify people groups among whom the gospel can be spread without encountering much barriers of understanding. Therefore, in Christ's gospel, people groups in our communities, country sides and wherever, can be described as the people outside the Kingdom of God.

The grim reality of whole groups of people in danger of perdition and without opportunity to receive a clear gospel witness should hasten all Churches to pray and recruit men and women provided with needful assistance who will make it possible to reach the unreached people where they live. These are people who have no church or any significant evangelistic or mission work done among them. In Mark 13:10, the Bible says, *"And the gospel must first be preached among all nations."* This speaks about people groups who are to be reached for Christ.

According to Bible dictionary, the Greek "ETHNOS" is translated "NATIONS." In our Bible, it can be translated as "ethnic groups or tribes." Hence, there are nations within nations. All unreached people groups fit into one nation or the other and can be found in the city/ village, province/state, or nation. It is necessary to find out in our community, region, or country where the unreached people groups live. Proverbs 18:15 says that, *"The heart of the prudent getteth knowledge; and the ear of the wise seeketh knowledge."* Spying out the land of a people groups is like the work of a detective looking for evidences that will lead him to find the solution to a problem. Some information bring more understanding and lead further to more discoveries.

There are some people to concentrate on by finding out their resources, making accurate inventory of the church before work starts and checking on the spiritual state of the people group, their strongholds, weaknesses, cultures, history, economy, politics, sociology, religions, idols, opinion leaders; and finding out if the people are open to the gospel. Will they respond? Will they readily accept the gospel?

Another groundwork includes finding out the method which will produce maximum results in terms of converts, conservation and establishment in the church of God. What has God begun to do among the people? What way is the Spirit of God moving in the community?

The location of unreached people, population trends and societal interest will provide more clarity in planting churches. We will also need to know what God is doing among the people and how the Holy Spirit is preparing them for the great harvest.

1

THE PRIORITY OF EVANGELISM IN CHURCH GROWTH

*A*nd Saul was consenting unto his death. And at that time there was a great persecution against the church which was at Jerusalem; and they were all scattered abroad throughout the regions of Judaea and Samaria, except the apostles...Therefore they that were scattered abroad went everywhere preaching the word...The woman then left her waterpot, and went her way into the city, and saith to the men, Come, see a man, which told me all things that ever I did: is not this the Christ? Then they went out of the city, and came unto (Jesus) him!" (Acts 8:1, 4; John 4:28-30).

Should we pray for this kind of persecution that would enable us to obey the Master Jesus? NO! The Church of Christ is predestined to grow both spiritually and numerically. As the insignificant point-size mustard seed grows into a gigantic leafy tree, so is the Church from an insignificant proportion divinely predestined to grow into a big Kingdom of innumerable saints. Yet, this growth does not come by chance. Church growth is achieved through a set of definite sustained inputs. Chief among these inputs is personal evangelism as revealed through a woman at the well in the Gospel of John chapter 4 with her personal encountered with Jesus. It is certainly the fastest, surest and cheapest means of church growth.

As stated by C. Austin Miles, "If you'll bring the one next to you, and I bring the one next to me, in no time at all we'll have them all, so win them, win them, one by one." Personal evangelism is systematic evangelistic outreaches handled and managed by an individual (born again Christian). It is, more or less, a one-man evangelistic thrust and in most cases, directed at one individual sinner at a time. Its purpose is to bring the sinner into a personal experimental knowledge of Jesus Christ as his/her Lord and Saviour. It is not just to accept a particular creed or join a particular church. It is not to be preached with bias or prejudice against anyone or any group of people. It should be targeted at all mankind. Although, the strategy of our outreaches may differ, the goal should be uniform - to bring souls of different persuasions into the Kingdom of God.

Repentance and remission of sin are essential elements of true gospel preaching. To shift the burden of man's salvation upon God without the commitment of the sinner is erroneous. It is the responsibility of every sinner to personally repent of his sins and exercise faith in the sacrifice of Christ before he could receive pardon.

Finally, our preaching aims at reconciling the sinner to God and not merely making religious zealots of them (2 Corinthians 5:18-21).

The Command of Master Jesus

The Lord Jesus Christ's commands in Matthew 28:19-20 is to "Go ye therefore, and teach all nations, baptizing them in the name of the Father, and of the Son, and of the Holy Ghost: Teaching them to observe all things whatsoever I have commanded you: and, lo, I am with you always, even unto the end of the world. Amen." A soldier acts on the command or orders of his superior officer. Therefore, every true Christian should evangelize. The command hinges on the urgency of the mission because the fields are white already to harvest (John 4:35).

The command of the Master of the house when His message was ignored by His own stock was that His servants should "... go out quickly into the streets and lanes of the city, and bring in hither the poor, and the maimed, and the halt, and the blind. And the servant said, Lord, it is done as thou hast commanded, and yet there is room. And the lord said unto the servant, Go out into the highways and hedges, and compel them to come in, that my house may be filled" (Luke 14:21-23).

The Lord, upon whose shoulders there shall be all governments, sees evangelism as the greatest need of the hour because an average of one hundred and five people die every minute, thousands of people die each day, while millions of people pass away into Christless eternity every week of the year.

(https://www.thegospelcoalition.org/article/105-people-die-each-minute/). Therefore, the Great Commission is binding on all born-again Christians. The command says, "go" but most church leaders and members want sinners to 'come' to them to hear them preach the gospel, the beautiful sermon from their pulpits.

We are called to be fishers of men, not to remain in the comfort of our swimming pool and expect fish to come. We are to go into all the world of men and women, the world of youths and adults, the world of literates and illiterates, the world of the rich and the poor, the world of workers and unemployed to preach the gospel of Christ. Our work is not done yet until we have been able to preach the gospel to the entire world around us. Preaching the gospel is more than making a person a member of the church or convincing him/her to stop a peculiar habit. In the Old Testament, God told Jonah to arise and *go unto Nineveh, that great city, and preach unto it (Jonah 3:2).* In like manner, we are to obey our Lord Jesus Christ and preach in the city and on the streets.

Until the preaching turns people from sin unto righteousness and holiness, the Great Commission is not yet done. Therefore, we need to preach the gospel, not our denomination or fables. After they have been won to the Lord, then we need to teach them to observe all things commanded by the Lord. We are to teach the new converts all the doctrines of the Bible to help them in faith and make disciples of them for Jesus.

The preaching of the gospel (on a personal scale) is a debt every true Christian owes sinners. This debt must be paid! We are debtors both to the Greeks, and to the Barbarians; both to the wise, and to the unwise (Romans 1:14; Read Ezekiel 33:7-9). The Lord Jesus demonstrated this example for us to follow by personally preaching to one Samaritan woman and He seems to be saying we should also do what we see Him (John 14:12). Every born-again Christian is duty bound to carry out this Great Commission as Jesus also came to seek and save that which was lost. Who are the lost? They are the people created by God to show forth His pleasure on earth but are now manifesting the works of the flesh (Luke 19:10; Galatians 5:19-21; 1 Corinthians 6:9-10).

Jesus came into this world because of the burden He had for humanity. His concern took Him through the nooks and crannies, seeking the dejected, the forsaken, the sick and lonely (Matthew 9:36). His compassion made Him shed His Blood on the cross of Calvary. He died to proclaim the gospel of liberty and said, "It is finished" (John 19:30). Through His vicarious death, lost humanity can be restored and reconciled to God the Creator, the Father of all. The question is – Has He brought you from the dungeon of sin and self? If yes, has He found you a kinsman? How about the people you meet every day as you go out and come in?

Who Can Preach?
Not everybody is qualified to preach the gospel. Those who wish to preach about Christ must have a personal experience of salvation in Christ Jesus, become His true

follower, live according to His precepts, be holy and at peace with all men. God Himself declared: "That he would grant unto us, that we being delivered out of the hand of our enemies might serve him without fear, In holiness and righteousness before him, all the days of our life... Depart ye, depart ye, go ye out from thence, touch no unclean thing; go ye out of the midst of her; be ye clean, that bear the vessels of the Lord" (Luke 1:74-75; Isaiah 52:11). God has made holy living possible through the death of Christ. The same blood that produces salvation in us has the ability to transform us entirely through sanctification.

It is very possible for a Christian in a miry world to single himself out and determine to live righteously. Holiness is meant for the redeemed of God, those believers who are truly born again. A Christian who is holy has victory over sin and the world. He puts love into action and manifests the fruit of the Spirit. He is kind, compassionate, easy to be entreated, not envious or proud. Holiness is a priority because it is the condition for seeing God after our journey here on earth (Hebrews 12:14). For a believer to be holy, he must be separated from the world. He must have a clean cut from sin in every shape and form. He must do away with everything that grieves the Holy Spirit which things cripple his spiritual life. He must dedicate his life fully to the Lord and be prayerful.

Holiness is not man-made; it is the work of God. It is not achieved by feelings; it is received through faith in Christ. Moreover, the Lord promised that "Ye shall receive power, after that the Holy Ghost is come upon you: and ye shall be witnesses unto me both in Jerusalem, and in all Judaea, and in Samaria, and unto the uttermost part of the earth" (Acts 1:8).

God is not a man that He should lie; whatever He has promised in His word shall be accomplished. Hence, every saved believer should thirst and hunger to be empowered and persevere through prayer with faith in God to operate in the power of Holy Ghost. This is because it is not possible to preach with the enticing worlds of man's wisdom and have a fruitful service which can only be achieved by the demonstration of the Holy Spirit's power.

The deplorable condition of these sinners and their impending doom should motivate us as believers to wait on God's power for Spirit-anointed preaching and ministering. We must be empowered before we can bring deliverance to the captives especially when they can see the manifestation of God's miraculous power to solve their problems that have been driving them from the pillar to post. We just must plunge into this power of God if we are ever going to be of help to them and depopulate hell.

Therefore, the true gospel preacher has the qualification of genuine salvation from sin and living in holiness through the Holy Ghost baptism which is needed for greater effectiveness and fruitfulness. In addition, we should emulate Christ in submission, consecration and commitment to the Great Commission. Philippians 2:5-11 revealed to us that our Lord Jesus Christ is the perfect example of a Christian in the service of God. Even though he was co-equal with the Father, He emptied Himself of His glory and totally submitted Himself to His Father's will. His submission was total, He submitted to the point of death.

Christ's life revealed to us submission, consecration and commitment to the Father's business. It was His submission that made Him say, "Not my will but thine be done." He yielded His life to His Father's service when he said, "My meat is to do the will of Him that sent me, and to finish His work" (John 4:34). From the text, the following characteristics are evident in Christ for us to emulate:

He consecrated Himself to the Father.
He laid aside His glory and made Himself of no reputation.

He took the form of a servant (slave).

He came in the likeness of man.

He humbled Himself.

He became obedient unto death.

In general, preachers of the gospel should live above reproach. A preacher with questionable lifestyle cannot hold out in ministry with success for a long time. As a result, every believer in Christ is self-sacrificing (laying all the altar of sacrifice), prompt and implicit in obedience to God's word, willing and read to serve, consistent, enduring hardship, free from worldly entanglements, self-controlled and Heaven-minded. You are also called to be a chosen generation, a royal priesthood, a holy nation, a peculiar people, that you should show forth the praises of Him who hath called you out of darkness into His marvellous light (1 Peters 2:9).

Consequently, we should publish the good news everywhere so as to bring growth to the church. Can others see in Jesus in you? Then, you are the one chosen to preach the gospel of the Kingdom of God and carry out this Great Commission. You do not need to wait for some kind of special ceremonial ordination before preaching the gospel.

In addition, the moral qualification of a gospel preacher cannot be overemphasized. It's not enough to be qualified as a preacher, there are moral qualities that are essentials to becoming a preacher in the church which are holiness in lifestyle, humility and harmlessness, hating of covetousness, honesty and good report, hospitality and benevolence, having a blameless home-life and neighbourliness.

Also, the following are needful qualities for gospel preachers:

Soul-winning passion (Acts 18:5; Romans 9:1-3).
Supplication spirit (Ephesians 6:18).
Shepherd's heart (Mark 6:34).
Scripture-saturated mind (Colossians 3:16).
Self-sacrificing life (Romans 16:3-4; Acts 20:24).
Simple and sound communication (Acts 18:28; 26:27-29).
Studying and diligent attitude (2 Timothy 2:15).

What we Preach
Upon the fall, man became sold under sin. He needs freedom from the penalty and consequences of sin; and only Jesus is the way, the truth, and the life without Whom no man shall inherit the Kingdom of God (John 14:6; Galatians 5:19-21).

The significance of the gospel message is Jesus Christ, Who died for the sins of the whole world. We should not preach sectarianism, doctrinal principles and Christian apologetics. Hence, the gospel should present the totality of Christ's sacrifice which has the power to save from sin. This, God has offered through salvation. It is disseminating the good tidings of the redemption of the world through the sacrificial death of Christ on the cross. All the benefits of Christ's redemptive work - forgiveness of sin and deliverance from its dominion and consequences - are conveyed through the instrumentality of the gospel.

The aim of our gospel preaching therefore is to make Christ known to all men as Saviour and Redeemer. Christ alone must be the subject of our discourse. In our gospel preaching, however, He should be projected and exalted in all His majesty, power, glory and as the only Saviour of the whole world (John 1:29; Acts 4:12). He is the Redeemer, who bought us back from the enemy's slave camp and as the Healer, He heals the sick and the broken-hearted (Luke 4:18; Acts 10:38). Not only that, He is the Deliverer. He offers the captives of Satan, the oppressed and afflicted, liberty and freedom; and gives sight to those physically or spiritually blind. Hence, Jesus Christ is the centrality of the gospel message to the perishing world.

The crucified Christ is the foundation of hope, fountain of joy and the hope of glory (Colossians 1:27). He also sheds light into our dark tunnel, brightens our horizon and illuminates our gloom. The realization of this aim should engage all our skills and energy. We are only to point to Jesus as the only resolution to life's conflicts. We are to describe man's sinful nature, warn the sinners about the impeding judgment of God, call for repentance from sins and advocate exercising of faith in Christ's work of atonement.

No matter the socialization, education and self-discipline, sin rules and reigns in the heart of every unregenerate sinner. All our self-righteousness is like a filthy rag in the sight of God. Sin will bring God's wrath and judgment upon every sinner because the wages of sin is death (Romans 6:23). To be free from sin and its consequences, every sinner must repent of his or her sins and be washed in the blood of Jesus (1 John 1:7) to be saved. The gospel is not only the story of Christ but Christ is the centrality of the gospel. Any preaching that fails to present Christ as the complete solution to sin is incomplete and therefore, cannot offer the full benefits of Christ's atonement.

Salvation from sin is possible only through Jesus Christ. There is no salvation outside of Christ (Acts 4:12). Through our Lord Jesus Christ alone, we obtain pardon and forgiveness of sin. Church attendance, involvement in religious activities, giving of alms, performance of rites (burning of candles, water baptism, taking Holy Communion) cannot earn sinners salvation.

To be saved, therefore, the sinner has to acknowledge his/her sins, confess and repent of every sin and accept Jesus Christ as his/her Lord and Saviour. Through His cross, our sins are paid for. His death on the cross, burial and resurrection are the crucial bases for our eternal life and redemption. If Christ has not been raised from the dead, the whole structure of the Christian faith and claim is shaken to its foundation. Christ's resurrection is the bedrock and distinguishing factor that marks out Christianity from other persuasions for eternal life. In His resurrection, the completeness of His work of atonement is demonstrated and confirmed. Therefore, the gospel message is the good news or glad tidings, the solemn message from God to men.

Where to Preach

We preach where the sinners are - in homes, streets, parks, market places, buses, trains and everywhere! The Lord says to go into all the world preaching and teaching the Gospel to every creature (Mark 16:15-16). Every believer's Jerusalem is their family, homestead or geographical location. Judea connotes neighbouring communities and states within a country. Samaria symbolises international missions while the uttermost parts of the earth is significant of the diaspora and intercontinental ministry to souls and people groups far away (Acts 1:8; Matthew 28:19-20).

Our duties are unlimited by racial, tribal, geographical and linguistic differences. Therefore, it is wrong and counter-productive to sit in the pews and hope to beckon sinners in. Christ came into the world to bring the world back to God. Similarly, we go into the world to bring the world back to Christ. Remember that Jesus told them again that as His Father sent Him, even so He sends us (John 20:21).

When to Preach
"Say not ye, There are yet four months, and then cometh harvest? behold, I say unto you, Lift up your eyes, and look on the fields; for they are white already to harvest...I must work the works of him that sent me, while it is day: the night cometh, when no man can work" (John 4:35; 9:5).

We preach now. We preach every time! The commandment has no time reference. As long as there is breathe in our nostrils, we preach the gospel. Every opportunity to preach should not be allowed to slip off. Preach the word. The task is urgent. It requires haste because the harvest of souls is plenteous (Matthew 9:36-37). The field is ripe and delay will result in colossal waste. The Master's message is urgent and must be carried out in haste.

The whole system is going down a crag. The signs of the Last Days as prophesized by our Lord and His apostles are being fulfilled before us. Morality and Godliness have been exchanged for full-fledged unrestrained depravity. Men and women have forgotten their Creator. It is important for us to arise urgently to rescue the lost before it is too late. The cost of delay would be immeasurable and the ripened harvest would be lost. When we consider the number of souls that slip into eternity every day, we should labour, depending on the Holy Spirit and Biblical methods to rescue the perishing souls. It is King's business. We must strive to please Him in this business.

Every born again soul should not allow the mundane things of this world to sidetrack him. Preach the word. If every Christian in the local church would preach the gospel to one sinner and win them in one month; and the converted sinner (now saint) would do the same thing and the cycle go unhindered, in just a few years, the world would be evangelized. The church will grow astronomically. The result would be more than one soul. Andrew found Peter, he brought him to Jesus (1 John 1:40-42).

How many souls did Peter win? Uncountable! All those souls won by Peter and the souls that all others won were all added to the church. No wonder, the early church has no problem with numerical growth. It grew naturally! World evangelization appears to be moving on the snail's speed and many pews are empty because the church is not serious with evangelism. It is high time each Christian engaged in personal evangelism with much compassion, personal prayer and seriousness so that the church can win the nations before the Lord returns (Romans9:1-3; 10:1).

Means of Growth

The reason for continuous mobilization of human and material resources for evangelization and expansion of the gospel work is that converts must be conserved, trained and deployed to continue the work among the people-group. There are many people groups yet to be reached, both home and abroad; and the time is short. It is high time each Christian arises, pulls down all barriers and engages in personal evangelism. May the Lord melt the saints and put us into circulation.

We saw the Samaritan woman leave her waterpot, and went into the city to invite men to come and see a man who told her all things she ever did; a man who gave her a dossier of her life and x-rayed her resume offhand.

She then quizzed them if this is not the Christ. "And many more believed because of his own word; And said unto the woman, Now we believe, not because of thy saying: for we have heard him ourselves, and know that this is indeed the Christ, the Saviour of the world" (John 4:28-29, 41-42).

Our world as today is complex and supplicated and there is not a single method sufficient and wise enough to make Christ's gospel known. Evangelizers must be creative, adapt, improvise and go beyond using orthodox means as usual.

2

STRATEGIES FOR PREACHER'S DEVELOPMENT

E very church worker, leader, pastor et al must, of necessity, have a vision for growth and development. He should see things as God sees them. This implies that he should be what God wants him to be and to do that, he has a part to play for he cannot be passive in this regard. For him to be effective on the pulpit and in the local assembly, he must carefully guard his private life. The greatness of his work and responsibilities and influence he exerts as a minister of God make his private life important. He must, therefore, do all things to keep himself a vessel fit for the Master's use at all times.

"That I may know him, and the power of his resurrection, and the fellowship of his sufferings, being made conformable unto his death; If by any means I might attain unto the resurrection of the dead. Not as though I had already attained, either were already perfect: but I follow after, if that I may apprehend that for which also I am apprehended of Christ Jesus. Brethren, I count not myself to have apprehended: but this one thing I do, forgetting those things which are behind, and reaching forth unto those things which are before, I press toward the mark for the prize of the high calling of God in Christ Jesus. Let us therefore, as many as be perfect, be thus minded: and if in anything ye be otherwise minded, God shall reveal even this unto you" (Philippians 3:10-15).

The moment a man receives pardon for sin through his faith in the atoning blood of Jesus Christ, he becomes a child in God's Kingdom. God bestows His grace on Him to grow spiritually while he must, on the other hand, be determined to grow. Every child desires the mother's milk for growth and it is only a sick child that rejects milk. In the same vein, every Christian should desire and hunger for the sincere milk of God's word for growth. Peter harped that, as newborn babes, a child of God must desire the sincere milk of the word that he may grow thereby (1 Peter 2:2).

Growth and development are necessary for all church workers to mature in the Lord and be adequately equipped for ministry. Leaders must avoid boredom, confusion and dissatisfaction in life and be approved as a workman that needed not to be ashamed. Church or ministry leaders need to have desired results in winning souls and maturing believers; and be a perfect example to members in the local church as Christ is to you in order to experience a fulfilled ministry. We have to abide in Christ up until the end and make it to Heaven at last.

Generally, church leaders and preachers are often tempted to believe they have arrived, but no one really arrives as this scripture shows. Our faith is progressive. Growth is normal in Christianity. Christ's Kingdom on earth does not admit stagnation. Progress is a feature of our belief system and limitations are abnormal. Growth, however, is systematic and depends on certain conditions. Our transition from one level or phase of spirituality and ministry to another is not automatic. Many Christians do not know this. Therefore, they do not advance. Such Christians risk eviction from the Kingdom (Hebrews 6:7-8). God frowns at Christians who flourish in stagnation and may order that they be severed from the main Vine (John 15:1-2).

Many Christians, even some so-called leaders and preachers, remain babyish because they do not work hard for their personal development. Some remain bound to the first level of redemption so that people wonder at this dormancy and begin to question their salvation. Some Christians pitch their spiritual tent at the bus stop of self-indulgence, living with the assumption that the Holy Spirit will align on them and fill them up with His anointing whenever He chooses to do so. They do not passionately thirst after Him with sustainable importunate prayers. As regards character growth, many Christians still maintain first-grader's behaviour years after their conversion and commission simply because they do not seem to care.

Let no one be deceived; every Christian should strive to attain all-round spiritual, character and ministerial growth. You must desire it, thirst for it, seek it and work for it. Otherwise, the Kingdom may spew you out. "I know thy works, that thou art neither cold nor hot: I would thou wert cold or hot. So then because thou art lukewarm, and neither cold nor hot, I will spue thee out of my mouth" (Revelation 3:15-16).

Personal development relates to the development of our own spirituality for lasting Christianity and better performance in the Lord service. It is personal because it pertains to you and I and it is something we must initiate and work out by ourselves. You may have access to sound and deep teaching and belong to a praying dynamic church. You may have a good Bible, a concordance, an array of Christian literature and commentaries. Anointed and prophetic messages are simply inputs of growth that we should grab and apply to foster our own development purpose in life (Joshua 1:8; Read 2 Timothy 2:15).

Personal development is not a selective improvement of one's Christianity. It is an integrated growth effort. Specially, it focuses on our knowledge of the God's Word, ministerial abilities, prayer life, character growth and faith level. The first essential is learning at the feet of the 'fathers.' The apostles, prophets, evangelists, pastors and teachers are given by the Holy Spirit to the Church for the perfecting of the saints, for the work of the ministry, for the edifying of the body of Christ: till we all come in the unity of the faith, and of the knowledge of the Son of God, unto a perfect man, unto the measure of the stature of the fulness of Christ: that we henceforth be no more children, tossed to and fro, and carried about with every wind of doctrine, by the sleight of men, and cunning craftiness, whereby they lie in wait to deceive" (Ephesians 4:12-14).

The ministers are placed over the church to feed the sheep, but if the sheep refuse feeding, what can the minister do? Those who don't attend fellowship regularly or special church programs won't derive any growth benefit from the various ministries in their church and such Christians will remain 'baby Christians' if at all they continue in faith (Hebrews 10:25).

The second essential thing is personal study of the Bible and other useful Scriptural literature and sermons. Those who don't study God's Word and His saints' writings cannot develop spiritually. Regular devotional study of God's Word serves as the chief means of obtaining an all-round spiritual development. It must be noted that personal development is a continuous process in every area of the life of a Christian. We must, therefore, study and meditate on the Scriptures daily in order to experience continuous personal development in our lives and ministry.

Apart from normal quiet time, there should be scheduled hours for consistent private study of God's Word and keeping strictly with them. In addition, books are the most important tools of the pastor/minister's calling. Good books will stimulate the pastor's thinking, develop his spirituality and keep him growing. The minister's library should be a rich library, one having a selection of basic books and covering various topics and areas of study. Such a selection should include Bibles, such as Thompson Chain-Reference Bible;" concordances such as Strong's Exhaustive Bible Concordance, Bible dictionaries and atlases such as International Standard Bible Encyclopedia, Unger's Bible Dictionary, and Baker's Bible Atlas. Bible study/sermon helps, commentaries, such as Matthew Henry's Commentary on the Whole Bible, Pulpit Commentary, Adam Clarke's Commentary on the Bible, among others. Therefore, the success or failure on the pulpit is determined by the attention the minister gives to his study. Faithful and continued study habits will result in a constructive and growing preaching ministry.

The third essential element of personal development is consistent personal prayer and devotional life. "And in the morning, rising up a great while before day, he went out, and departed into a solitary place, and there prayed... Pray without ceasing" (Mark 1:35; 1 Thessalonians 5:17). Effective prayer begins with worship, praises and thanksgiving unto God (Matthew 6:9), before intercession and, lastly asking for our needs. Jesus Christ our Lord is our perfect example in living a regular prayer life. He started and ended the day with prayers. Likewise, He commanded us to pray continually (Luke 18:1). Those who depend on congregational prayers and devotions but seldom call on the Father of creation and commune with Him alone will only, at best, experience slow and minimal growth.

Check the scriptures and church history, great saints and servants of God were all men and women who wrestle with God alone in secret prayer. Most development efforts will be useless without regular prayer support. Spiritual gifts and revelations come through prayers (Acts 10:9-10; Revelations 1:9-10). Surely, it isn't in vain that the Bible counsels us to pray without ceasing. Prayer is a defence mechanism and catalyst of growth. As a result, the pastor, in particular, has a ministry of intercession which cannot be denied. We live in a deceived world, a dangerous world, a defied world and a divided world. Members of local churches have to contend with this world, therefore every pastor ought to intercede for the members of his church. "O that one (even the pastor) might plead for a man with God, as a man pleadeth for his neighbour!" (Job 16:21).

The fourth essential means of Christian development is practice – that is using the gifts and knowledge we have received in our daily living in the Lord's service. Spiritual materials get better with use. God adds more grace to the believer's abilities for using what he has for God's glory. Those who don't use the grace they have lose it and then relapse into mediocrity. We shouldn't be afraid to take faith-risks; we shouldn't dodge assignments if we desire to develop. Dodgers don't develop.

Above all, he who desires to develop must aspire for it. You should hate stagnation and be discontent with low-level Christianity if you want to grow. Developed Christians possess the spiritual characteristics of 'adult' believers. They are not babyish in knowledge, wisdom, character, ability and power. They are ever ready for the Lord's service and demonstrate self-discipline, sobriety, deep spiritual stability, consistency, consecration and commitment. It should be known that development is a continuous thing; no one ever reaches the point at which further development becomes unnecessary. Until we depart from the earth, we will never cease from pressing forward because the moment we stop to grow we begin to die.

Power For Effective Soulwinning

If there is any time when preachers, pastors, evangelists, prophets, church leaders or servants of God should rise up for fruitful service, it is now. This is because we are living in the days of apostasy when people are deviating from the purpose of God and many are becoming more religious than righteous. It is time when the love of many Christians is waxing cold and sinners are growing stronger and stronger in their sins. Thus, only the demonstration of God's power, not the shallow life, can deliver them. God is not a man that should lie; whatever He has promised in His Word shall be accomplished and He can never send His servants on a fool's errand or on a mission without giving them His power to accomplish the mission. Moses had a rod, Joshua had the decrees and the early disciples of Christ had the Holy Spirit and His giftings. The Lord says ye shall receive power and that settles it (Luke 24:27-29; Acts 1:8; Micah 3:8).

No preacher has any excuse for mediocrity and failure in spiritual warfare. The Lord says, "I send the promises of my Father upon you." If the Father anointed Jesus for the mission, then, we are anointed too! and the work He did, He has promised we too will do... and greater works! Hence, winning souls effectively for Christ is more than calling a person into the church gathering. It is more than convincing an individual that Christianity is a good religion.

Soulwinning turns those who are deep in sins to righteousness and holiness. It is not possible to preach with enticing word of man's wisdom and have a fruitful soulwinning. Soulwinning cannot be accomplished without divine assistance. It's only by the demonstration of the Spirit and power of God. The wretched condition of sinners and their impending doom should motivate us as Christians to wait on God's power for Spirit-anointed preaching and ministering. The power of the Holy Spirit is indispensable in the soulwinner's life. The degree of his efficacy and fruitfulness is determined by this all-important experience.

The Holy Spirit is able to make the work successful now as in the days of Apostles because Jesus is the same yesterday, today and forever (Hebrews 13:8). The Holy Spirit can bring in souls by hundreds and thousands as well as in ones and twos.

The reason we are no more prosperous in soulwinning is that we do not have the Holy Spirit in us (in His might and power) as in early times. It is the extra-ordinary power from God and not talent or mental power. Mental power may fill a chapel but spiritual power will save souls. What we need is spiritual power. This, therefore, calls for preachers empowered of God to be able to carry out a fruitful service. It is futile to seek to replace the power of God with man-made strategies; only the power of God in a servant of God can make for fruitful service. The battle of liberating sinners from the clutches of sin is a spiritual warfare and only those who are spiritually equipped can be used of God. Such will not only be fruitful but will also find joy in their service for the Lord.

Even though there is need for a preacher to be empowered for God's service, it is utmost importance that his heart is made pure before power comes. Power without purity is dangerous and deceptive as it makes such a person a powerful fool. It is only the power of God that can purify the heart and make holy living possible. Every preacher who is a recipient of the miracle of salvation by grace is admonished to press further, thirst and pray always to remain saved, which is the sanctification experience otherwise known as purity of heart and holiness of life. The life of a Christian leader in particular is an epistle before the eyes of others (2 Corinthians 3:2-3). He should live a challenging, model life of transparent honesty, spotless conduct and integrity.

This is what God demands from preachers who carry the vessels of the Lord (Isaiah 52:11) with gospel proclamation. "Depart ye, depart ye, go ye out from thence, touch no unclean thing; go ye out of the midst of her; be ye clean, that bear the vessels of the LORD." For us to be vibrant for God, we need purity of life. This will make us blameless, honest, faithful and disciplined in life and service.

Furthermore, for the preacher who sincerely desires the Holy Spirit baptism, the numerous promises of God's willingness to give and His provision for this experience give a solid basis for earnest seeking for it.

"And it shall come to pass afterward, that I will pour out my spirit upon all flesh; and your sons and your daughters shall prophesy, your old men shall dream dreams, your young men shall see visions: And also upon the servants and upon the handmaids in those days will I pour out my spirit" (Joel 2:28-29).

Moreover, we know that the Scripture cannot be broken. The mighty outpouring of the God's Spirit is promised to "all flesh" and everyone who meets God's condition can receive God's abundance of the promised Spirit. From Scriptural examples, the initial sign and external evidence of the Holy Spirit baptism is speaking in tongues. However, receiving the Holy Spirit is more than just speaking in tongues. The power of God that accompanies that experience equips the believers to do the great exploits for the Lord.

There are many who claim to have the Holy Spirit baptism, yet, the power is conspicuously missing in their lives and ministry. Supernatural power is associated with the Holy Spirit. The power, however, is not to be used for personal or selfish purposes. We should emulate the example of our Lord Jesus Christ, "How God anointed Jesus of Nazareth with the Holy Ghost and with power: who went about doing good, and healing all that were oppressed of the devil; for God was with him" (Acts 10:38).

The power was mightily present in Christ and with that power, He ministered to save the lost and met divers needs in the lives of multitudes. The apostles in the early church received the power of the Holy Spirit, evangelized and also performed miracles that led multitudes to salvation in Christ. This is the major reason we need the power of the Holy Spirit today.

The power of the Holy Spirit can accomplish the following in a believer's life:

The Holy Spirit equips the believer to resist the devil and gives victory in the time of temptation (John 14:26; Romans 8:2).

The Holy Spirit empowers the believer to do fruitful services for the Lord (Read 1 Corinthians 12:7-11).

He helps the believers in prayers – "Likewise the Spirit also helpeth our infirmities: for we know not what we should pray for as we ought: but the Spirit itself maketh intercession for us with groanings which cannot be uttered. And he that searcheth the hearts knoweth what is the mind of the Spirit, because he maketh intercession for the saints according to the will of God" (Romans 8:26-27; Read Zechariah 12:10).

The Holy Spirit illuminates, inspires, and reveals the deep things of God to the believers. "Howbeit when he, the Spirit of truth, is come, he will guide you into all truth: for he shall not speak of himself; but whatsoever he shall hear, that shall he speak: and he will shew you things to come. He shall glorify me: for he shall receive of mine, and shall shew it unto you" (John 16:13-15; Read 1 Corinthians 2:9-12).

The Holy Ghost guides the believer into all truths (John 14:26; 15:26; 16:13) and He comforts and counsels believers – "And the spirit of the LORD shall rest upon him, the spirit of wisdom and understanding, the spirit of counsel and might, the spirit of knowledge and of the fear of the LORD" (Isaiah 11:2; Read Acts 13:2).

The Holy Spirit also equips believers with the fruit of the Spirit. "But the fruit of the Spirit is love, joy, peace, longsuffering, gentleness, goodness, faith, Meekness, temperance: against such there is no law" (Galatians 5:22-23).

The resultants effects of the enduement of Holy Spirit power are marvelous - conviction of sin, wisdom in communication, boldness and courage in preaching with coherency of texts and statements, exaltation of Christ, challenging victory over spiritual attack and anointing on the message. What we need is spiritual power.

Every saved and sanctified believer is eligible to receive the power of Holy Ghost at baptismal measure. God does not lie but always fulfills whatever He has promised and His word shall be accomplished. There is an urgent need for every believer to receive the infilling power of the Holy Ghost because the harvest is now plenteous but the labourers are few. Hence, it is God's perfect will for earnest seekers that are saved to live in the fullness of the Holy Ghost.

Preachers' Spiritual Gifts In Gospel Proclamation

"Now concerning spiritual gifts, brethren, I would not have you ignorant... But the manifestation of the Spirit is given to every man to profit withal" (1 Corinthians 12:1, 7). Ignorance is so costly; so dangerous! With respect to spiritual gifts, ignorance makes the Christian a weakling on the battle field, most especially, in evangelistic outreaches.

If one isn't aware that God, by His Spirit, has provided the means of winning the invisible war for the work of His Kingdom, one will defencelessly fight on relying on weak weapons to square it up with an enemy who has the most sophisticated arsenal in spiritual existence.

The result of such war can best be imagined and a lot of casualties of spiritual warfare are first victims of ignorance because they lack the knowledge of the existence of gifts of the Spirit which are meant to be applied in warfare to make victory smooth and sure.

"Now there are diversities of gifts, but the same Spirit. And there are differences of administrations, but the same Lord. And there are diversities of operations, but it is the same God which worketh all in all. But the manifestation of the Spirit is given to every man to profit withal. For to one is given by the Spirit the word of wisdom; to another the word of knowledge by the same Spirit; To another faith by the same Spirit; to another the gifts of healing by the same Spirit; To another the working of miracles; to another prophecy; to another discerning of spirits; to another divers kinds of tongues; to another the interpretation of tongues: But all these worketh that one and the selfsame Spirit, dividing to every man severally as he will" (1 Corinthians 12:4-11).

Many people deny both the existence of the gifts and their relevance in the modern church. Some so-called leaders (who thought they are doing God's work and value their position above God's act) in the congregation craftily stir up the fire of persecution against gifted brothers and sisters which would force their exit from the church. However, the Gospel truth is that the gifts exist and are being put to profitable use by those who have them and the knowledge of their appropriate application. We shouldn't be ignorant about the gifts.

The Holy Spirit owns the gifts and gives them to the Christians. All Christians are entitled to the gifts but the Holy Spirit decides which gift He gives each Christian with which to edify the church of the living God. Yet, a Christian may have all the gifts. The gifts are given to be used profitably to the glory of God. They are not toys or means for personal ego-boosting. They aren't possessions to be flaunted or bragged about.

In the Church, the operation of the gifts is to be controlled and their usefulness wisely applied (Please, read 1 Corinthians 14 for details). The gifts are nine in number and are classified into three groups thus:

Revelation: Word of knowledge, Word of wisdom, Discerning of spirits. **Power**: Faith, Healing and Miracles. **Vocal**: Prophecy, Diverse tongues, Interpretation of tongues.

The full details of these nine gifts are explained in one of my books - *Victorious Christian Living Essentials*.

In Luke 13:10-13, we could see that satan had bound the woman for eighteen years. Thank God for Jesus! The gifts of the Spirit can be applied as weapons of war in spiritual battles. Some of these gifts are indispensable war weapons. Without them, the enemy will appear more invincible and too difficult to track down. The revelational gifts expose the enemy's strategies, his extent of strength and subtle operational techniques. The word of knowledge reveals the unknown and unravel mysteries. The word of wisdom may be applied in tactical formulation of battle plans based on the secrets got through the word of knowledge. The gift of discerning spirits makes it impossible for the enemies to disguise, lay ambush and launch attacks without detection.

Faith blocks off the enemy's fiery darts of temptation and the gift of healing and working of miracles enable the Christian to storm the enemy's gulag and set the captives free. While the battle rages on, the gift of prophecy helps console the wounded, comfort the troubled and encourage the weak. At the same time, the gifts of diverse tongues and interpretation confer the opportunity of a wide range of prayer-type on the believer, making him more powerful and lethal. By the same gift, he props up his courage and confidence through the experience of edification. How can the saints of God be perfected if any of these gifts is missing or if we deliberately disallow its operation because of counterfeit preachers, false teachers and fake prophets all around us? We can never be wiser than the Giver (Holy Spirit) of the gifts.

The fact that there are many false gifts outside doesn't rule out the true gifts of the Holy Spirit in the Kingdom. Some leaders in the church pretentiously and deliberately disallow the use of the spiritual gifts so as not to expose their evil deeds; and they are afraid of young leaders whom they thought could displace them in their leadership positions. Hence, they look for flimsy excuses and lie deliberately against such persons in order to send them packing. But the Lord is sounding a warning to take heed unto yourselves, and to all the flock, over the which the Holy Ghost hath made you overseers, to feed the church of God, which he hath purchased with his own blood (Acts 20:28). May God deliver His Church from such selfish leaders who value their positions more than the state of the flocks of Christ in Jesus' mighty name.

In Ephesians 4:11-16; "And he gave some, apostles; and some, prophets; and some, evangelists; and some, pastors and teachers; For the perfecting of the saints, for the work of the ministry, for the edifying of the body of Christ: Till we all come in the unity of the faith, and of the knowledge of the Son of God, unto a perfect man, unto the measure of the stature of the fulness of Christ: That we henceforth be no more children, tossed to and fro, and carried about with every wind of doctrine, by the sleight of men, and cunning craftiness, whereby they lie in wait to deceive; But speaking the truth in love, may grow up into him in all things, which is the head, even Christ: From whom the whole body fitly joined together and compacted by that which every joint supplieth, according to the effectual working in the measure of every part, maketh increase of the body unto the edifying of itself in love"

The great Apostle Paul disclosed in our text that when our Jesus Christ ascended into Heaven, He distributed the ministry gifts to some believers to function as apostles, prophets, evangelists, pastors and teachers. These gifts are different from personal spiritual gifts.

They are referred to as five-fold ministry gifts for ministers which the Holy Spirit gives to the church to develop the members, help them to discover and use their personal spiritual gifts for the benefit of church growth and development. The purpose of the gifts in the church is to ginger edification, grow saints and equipped them for the work of God in the ministry. He expects members to reach spiritual levels of mature believers that would be able to stand in the face of the challenges and deceits of the world. These foster love and unity among believers and increase our knowledge of Jesus and His Kingdom.

Apostles are messengers called directly by Jesus Christ and given special authority to lay doctrinal foundation in the church and to monitor the growth of the assembly from one place to the other.

The prophet is gifted to speak unto men for comfort, edification, exhortation. They are heart revealers, and supernaturally enabled to receive and reveal God's will for His people wherever they go. They miraculously see the past, the present and future events.

The evangelist is specially gifted to preach. He is a carrier of the Good news that point sinners to Christ and challenge fellow believers to win souls.

The pastor is a soul healer who watches over the souls in his care. He gently exhorts, warns and comforts them in divine service. As a shepherd, he orders the worship, church administration and preaching the Word of God to the congregation.

The teacher edifies the church, touches the intellect of the people and imparts knowledge about God through His Word. He's divinely empowered with a supernatural ability to communicate and clarify the details of God's Word clearly and to lead the flock to God. All teachers may not necessarily be pastors, but all pastors should be teachers of God's Holy Word.

God's purpose for His people is to grow in love and come to unity and perfection in Christ (Ephesians 4:13). Therefore, all believers in Christ should desire the full stature of Christ's unity of faith, love and holiness. This is the only way we can become productive members of the Body of Christ in winning souls and wreaking havoc on the kingdom of darkness (John 15:2; Luke 11:13).

Leonard Ravenhill, as passionately as he could manage, exhorted the Christian to get empowered. He wrote, "With all thy getting, get auction." Too many Christians carry on in the faith without any apparent desire to be spirit-filled and operate in the giftings of the Holy Spirit. The battle is getting hotter as the Lord's arrival gets closer. Satan is putting his whole arsenal into this battle with greater desperation, ruthlessness and blood-thirstiness.

No Christian can afford to tag along without the power and special grace of the Holy Spirit. To do so is to court disaster. In 1 Corinthians 12:31, Apostle Paul admonished us to covet earnestly the best gifts. That is the strongest language in saying, don't rest, don't get satisfied, don't feel at ease until the Holy Spirit begins to operate His gifts in you. Until you are baptized with the Holy Spirit power, you cannot be ushered into the experience of the operations of spiritual gifts. Please, for God's sake and His Kingdom:

Thirst for the gifts.
Ask for the gifts.
Play the service roles that call for the gifts.
Believe and act them out in faith.
The battle has begun - Shell the enemy to:

Free the captured saints
Save the helpless sinning souls
Heal the hopelessly sick
Deliver the oppressed
Bless the poor

Therefore, prayer should be habitual, ceaseless, spiritual, fervent and faith-propelled to regain the lost grounds of spiritual strength, clear vision, Scripture knowledge, inspiration and prosperity because the battle is hot and continuous,.

3

DEFENSIVE AND OFFENSIVE WEAPONS OF PREACHERS

A postle Paul, by the Spirit of the Lord, has been talking to the Ephesian church in this epistle. In five chapters, he has talked about their special calling by God's grace, commended their faith, prayed for their spiritual growth and strengthening, assured them of their glorious position in Christ and exhorted them on holiness and proper Christian conduct. Now, in chapter 6 verse 10, he is closing up with a call to get armed for battle!

All exhortations, teachings and discipling will be futile if the Christian is not put on red alert for battle. We need to know that there are wars to fight and be told what weapons we need, lest the enemy swoop on us unawares.

In no other area of spiritual activity is the whole armour more necessary than in preaching and ministering deliverance. Haven't we heard of deliverance ministers who got injured in action? We've heard stories of demon transfer. All these wouldn't have been possible if the preachers or ministers had had the whole armour on.

In essence, Christianity is not a picnic affair. Our joy, singing and growth take place in the midst of fiery battles against principalities, powers, rulers, of the darkness of this world, and spiritual wickedness in high places. These are the hosts of hell that relentlessly attack our positions with the aim of halting our advancement in gospel's proclamations; and their intention is to destroy our strength and recapture our souls.

The Lord sums up the facts of the battle in Matthew 11:12, when He revealed that from the days of John the Baptist until now, the Kingdom of heaven involves or allows violence against sublime and tangible vices which must be violently resisted by the force of goodness, faith and a sense of spiritual responsibility. Heaven is not for chickens. It is for heroes of spiritual warfare. Why do we need the whole armour of God?

For we are wrestling against invisible foes in verse 12 of Ephesians chapter 6 and we won't be able to stand the destructive power of the enemy if we go into battle without the weapons in verse 13. Also, we had better get the weapons on because this battle must be fought. Every Christian is on the firing line; there's no room for lookers-on. You are either a fighting believer or a sinner bound up inside the enemy's dungeon.

We should know and put on the right weapons and armour or else, we will be easily defeated by enemies all of whom have the right weapons they need for the fight. Our reference names the weapons all of which could be classified thus:

Defensive Weapons (Ephesians 6:14-17).
These are weapons of defence in the battle field. They are:

Truth: This is integrity, honest assessment of our worth and admission of our weakness before the Lord. Leaning on the Lord in spiritual battles makes victory sure.

Breastplate of righteousness: This is practical holiness (1 Peter 1:15-17; Hebrews 12:14). Notice that the breastplate is worn on the chest inside which the heart is located. If the breastplate is missing, death becomes easier, swifter and surer. The unrighteous can't win spiritual battles.

Feet shod with the gospel (preaching): Witnessing for Christ is a defensive weapon and a protective device. Preaching involves confessions and assertions. There is awesome power in what we say often (Romans 10:9-10). So, witnessing Christians are, in a way, helping themselves!

Shield of faith: This is related to our belief in the invisible God whom we serve and on whose authority we to war. Without the shield of faith, we will overrate enemies, be terrified by their weapons and might ruthlessly lose the fight even before the first shot is fired.

Helmet of Salvation: The meaning of this weapon is clear. It is not enough to be saved from sin; we should always strive to ensure that we remain saved at all times. The symbol used to describe salvation here show that it is the most defensive weapon. The helmet is worn on the head, the most delicate part of the human body. An injury on the head is more deadly than one on any other body-part. If this weapon is missing, so-called believers become more vulnerable and won't have any chance of survival, let alone winning. Get born again and stay born again!

Offensive Weapons

These are weapons of attack. We do not only defend our gains in Christianity, we also push the enemies further back to capture more territories for the Lord. It takes both defensive and offensive fighting to win a battle. That is why we are enjoined to put on the whole or complete armour of God. Here are the offensive weapons:

The Sword of the Spirit – This is the Word of God, the totality of the inspired Scriptures. It is the chief offensive weapon with infinite power and application. With the Word, we shell the enemy's territories, weaken his strength, paralyze his operations, cut off his supply routes and knock him out of action. With the Sword of the Spirit, temptations, that is, the enemy's battle-tricks, are overcome with ease and lost grounds are recaptured. When properly applied, the sword sways both ways – defending the Christian and attacking the enemy's positions. Get the Word and use it well. It is your greatest weapon!

Spirit-filled prayer – The meaning of this is obvious. All kinds of prayers are a great arsenal in spiritual battles. Not this alone, prayers activates all other weapons. Without prayer, all the other weapons are impotent. Prayer kick-starts the weaponry and releasing their lethal potentialities. It is the trigger and works both to defend and attack. A prayerless or prayer-weak Christian will be numbered among the casualty or the dead. If God has mercy on him, he may survive to live in the enemy's dungeon as a prisoner of war until the battle is over at the rapture. Prayer should be part of us because the battle is hot and continuous.

4

CONSECRATION AND COMMITMENT FOR SOULWINNING

C onsecration and commitment are the essential factors and price of a successful Christian ministry. Commitment is the giving up of oneself or being totally sold to a course and refusing to be distracted by any opposing circumstances or hindrances on the way. This is strengthened by the level of consecration of the believer. The more consecrated one is, the more committed he becomes. Consecration is the laying of all we are and all we have on the altar of God. This is a pre-requisite for receiving spiritual blessings, equipment and anointing for a successful ministry. Moses told the Israelites to consecrate themselves to the Lord that he may bestow a blessing upon them (Exodus 32:29). It is the consecrated, foolish and weak things of this world that God uses to confound the wise and the mighty (1 Corinthians 1:26-29).

Therefore, the subject of commitment and consecration cannot be neglected without serious consequences as regards the ministry of the Church. Committed and consecrated preachers are always distinguished in their success and achievement in the work of the ministry. The work of God in these Last Days requires men and women of commitment whose daily joy is the progress of God's cause on earth.

Everything around us seems to be calling us into commitment to Christian service because of the ripened plenteous harvest of souls (Matthew 9:37-38; Read John 4:34-38); the limited period or shortness of time coupled with the unsaved multitudes who are in danger of eternal judgment (John 9:4); the great need of perfecting and maturing the saints in the church Ephesians 4:12-14); the increasing responsibility of feeding the flock of God (Acts 20:28) and the necessity of the continuity of God's work despite opposition from satan and his agents (Nehemiah 6:10-14).

Furthermore, the great challenges of being strong in the Lord and in the power of His might; keeping the standard of Christian living in this age of ecumenical movements (Ephesians 6:10); being able to finish our appointed ministries (Acts 20:19-24) and to making it to Heaven as well (2 Timothy 4:1-8) call for real commitment before the Great Commission can be carried out as the Lord expected and mandated. Without entire consecration, we cannot be fully committed to God's service; neither can we receive the power needed for service. This is why the call to consecration is unconditional and unavoidable. God requires that we give our hearts to him first (Proverbs 23:26).

Our bodies and all our substances are to be laid on the altar. Just as God required that all the firstborn of the redeemed Israelites are separated unto the Lord, all believers are to live consecrated and separated lives unto God. This will include the sacrificing of all personal ambition, desires, will and plans on the altar of God and the willingness to give up anything, if the Lord so requires. Why should we be consecrated?

God has all authority to demand our all as the Maker and Creator of all things. Besides this, He bought us and gave us a new life through the Lord Jesus Christ – eternal life. As parents have control over their children, so also, God has a right and control over us as His children, however dare His demands (Hebrews 12:9-11).

We are also bought with price. As owners have right over their properties, so likewise God has complete claim over us and all we are and all we have. Christ also, to Whom we are to be conformed, gave us an example of consecration. He gave up all and became poor that we, through His poverty, might be made rich. "For ye know the grace of our Lord Jesus Christ, that, though he was rich, yet for your sakes he became poor, that ye through his poverty might be rich" (2 Corinthians 8:9).

Moreover, consecration brings God's blessings, anointing and equipment upon us, but whatever we are consecrating to God must be free from sin (Ecclesiastes 10:1); separated unto God like a Nazarene (Numbers 6:2-3,13); purged from all leavens (1 Corinthians 5:3-11); broken or easily broken, conquered from all self-will, crucified to the world and the flesh and fully yielded and surrendered. In Numbers 32:12, the Bible says that Caleb the son of Jephunneh the Kenezite, and Joshua the son of Nun for they have wholly followed the Lord.

Therefore, the committed consecrated preacher or worker must maintain personal obedience to God irrespective of what others do such as Caleb and Joshua did. The pressure, disappointments, ridicule, criticism and wrong judgment of others cannot stop the committed preacher from doing the will of God.

The church worker who is committed to serving God's people can sacrifice his personal conveniences and food to observe fasting in order to obtain a breakthrough in difficult and dangerous times like Esther. The threats of the enemies never move him; he joyfully takes the spoiling of his goods and rejoices when he is maltreated or persecuted and suffers the loss of anything without bitterness.

Like Paul the Apostle, he counts all things but loss for the excellency of the knowledge of Christ Jesus. He labours tirelessly more than all others, yet he is humble in defending the truth of the gospel at all cost. He laid down his neck for his Master's service. The crown of righteousness waits such committed church workers and preachers. "I have fought a good fight, I have finished my course, I have kept the faith: Henceforth there is laid up for me a crown of righteousness, which the Lord, the righteous judge, shall give me at that day: and not to me only, but unto all them also that love his appearing" (2 Timothy 4:7-8).

The Power Of Love In Soulwinning

Our world is hungry for love. No one, saint or sinner, ever rejects love and care. Some feel so unloved and uncared for and therefore, decide to commit suicide or terrorism rather than continuing to live. Others prefer to be reserved and self-centered. Many find it impossible to single-handedly overcome dangers that two or more people could have conveniently handled.

In God's infinite wisdom, He chose the way of love to reach sinful humanity through His Son Jesus Christ (John 3:16). As a believer that has tasted the love of Calvary, you should look out to love and care for people. It is privilege to love and care for the weak and weary, the lonely and withdrawn, the destitute and discouraged, for all and sundry. The opportunity to help those you see today may not always be there and you may ever live to regret any lost opportunity to love the ones who need your love (Galatians 5:14).

Above all, another Christian quality greatly priced by God and men is fervent and unconditional love from the heart (1 Peter 1:22). When great faith, sound knowledge and high spirituality fail (1 Corinthians 13:1-3), as they sometimes do, try love in action, it can never fail! It is a contradiction to have Christians who live without love for the brethren and for others because love is the evidence of the new birth.

It is the impulse of the new convert. No wonder, a sinner cannot love as God expects until he fully surrenders the heart to the Lord Jesus at the cross. Then, the life and light of God will fill the heart with love.

Only the Lord Jesus can impact God's kind of love called the "agape" in our hearts. This divine love contradicts the false and inauthentic love expressed in selfishness, reward-seeking deeds, eye-service or hypocrisy, flattery and suspicion. In 1 Corinthians 13:4-7, Paul the apostle says, "Charity suffereth long, and is kind; charity envieth not; charity vaunteth not itself, is not puffed up, Doth not behave itself unseemly, seeketh not her own, is not easily provoked, thinketh no evil; Rejoiceth not in iniquity, but rejoiceth in the truth; Beareth all things, believeth all things, hopeth all things, endureth all things." Therefore:

I accept people as they are.
I believe people are valuable.
I care when others hurt.
I desire only what is best for others.
I erase all offences.

Of a truth, love is the most powerful ingredient that can touch and bless lives. It's more powerful than mere duty. Love is irresistible. Spontaneous and unconditional love is contagious and attracts people easily. (John 13:34-35). The practice of love in action takes a great deal of time and efforts but the dividends outweigh the personal cost. We must realize the tremendous value of each person in the body of Christ and in the neighbourhood and love them. As our walk with God becomes stronger, our ability to cultivate relationships with others will heighten.

There's nothing shallow about agape love. It bears all things, believes all things, hope all things, endure all things and never fails (1 Corinthians 13:7-8). It is the tough, enduring and resilient love. When the storms of life blow high and dangerous, genuine love for others does not retreat, rather, it seeks to wade through the storm, trusting in God to see it through. If we expect to make it through life and be effective in ministry, we dare not neglect love. The power of love is the power of evangelism to win the whole world unto Christ the Saviour (Matthew 5:13-16).

Love is practical Christianity. It is the possession of a natural tender and kindness as the divine. Life is made up not of great sacrifices or duties but of little deeds in which smiles and kindness rendered habitually will win and preserve the heart and comfort the hurting. The believer that does not do so is unjust. Love is an act of the will, a determination of the believer to make his or her life a sacrifice or gift to neighbours, colleagues, friends, persecutors to mention but a few. However, let us quickly warn that love is not expressed in feeling in but action. It is not only in emotion but in attitude.

It is not self-centered but people-centered. It is not in words but in deeds. It is love and kindness in a believer that can win others to the Lord and not just his deeds.

The first step to love is to identify the weak, confused, neglected, the destitute and the ones who need your affection. In a nutshell, make others happy. It is the only way for you to be holy, happy and healthy. Once you have embarked on the more excellent way, you will need to increase and strengthen your love as you seek the divine help of the Holy Spirit to touch lives through love and care.

Passion For Effective Soulwinning

"But when he saw the multitudes, he was moved with compassion on them, because they fainted, and were scattered abroad, as sheep having no shepherd. Then saith he unto his disciples, the harvest truly is plenteous, but the labourers are few; Pray ye therefore the Lord of the harvest, that he will send forth labourers into his harvest... Then flew one of the seraphims unto me, having a live coal in his hand, which he had taken with the tongs from off the altar: And he laid it upon my mouth, and said, Lo, this hath touched thy lips; and thine iniquity is taken away, and thy sin purged. Also, I heard the voice of the Lord, saying, whom shall I send,

and who will go for us? Then said I, Here am I; send me"
(Matthew 9:36-38; Isaiah 6:6-8).

Passion is active. It is a driving force that energizes and propels the consecrated believers to step out from their comfort zones and actively get involved in God's service. Spiritual passion happens when someone is looking up unto Jesus undistracted and walking side by side with Him up till date which brings a burning zeal, or deep-seated excitement and compassion that satisfies the soul. This cannot be experienced without a definite experience of salvation.

By passion for souls, it means earnest and strong desire and great concern to see sinners converted. It is exciting, manifesting and productive. The value of the soul and eternal destiny of those who are forever lost compel each believer to have the mind of Christ, go out and seek to save the lost every day. Every believer is charged with this responsibility of taking the good news to the sinful man. Such must have a deep, burning, Christ-like compassion which will compel him to sacrifice all that is necessary for the salvation of others.

A preacher once said, "The intensity of your compassion will be the measure of the sacrifice you make, of the effectual fervent prayer you offer, and of the long tireless journeys you make, of the tears you shed, of the earnest speeches and invitation to Christ you give and of the hardship you endure for the souls of men." The human soul is the battle ground between God and the devil. The soulwinner works with God against the devil to lead men, women and children to Christ and His Kingdom.

Life is short, eternity is nearer than ever, Jesus Christ our Lord will appear in a moment we least expect Him. Think about the fiery judgment of God awaiting the ungodly. It will be terrible! Therefore, we have to see these never-dying souls with eternity in view. See sinners as Jesus sees them; have some empathy because they are doomed for hell fire where there will be weeping and gnashing of teeth if they are not saved (Matthew 13:41-42).

Oh! What a loss and frustration of God's grace! It was to redeem these never-dying, priceless souls that Jesus left His position of honour and glory with the Father and came to this world to give His blameless life for our perverse lives to be reconciled to God. Survey the wondrous cross on which the Prince of glory died! and no price will seem too high to pay; no sacrifice too great to make; and no problem too big to encounter for the salvation of the lost.

Apostle Paul said. "I say the truth in Christ, I lie not, my conscience also bearing me witness in the Holy Ghost, That I have great heaviness and continual sorrow in my heart. For I could wish that myself were accursed from Christ for my brethren, my kinsmen according to the flesh..._Brethren, my heart's desire and prayer to God for Israel is, that they might be saved. For I bear them record that they have a zeal of God, but not according to knowledge. For they being ignorant of God's righteousness, and going about to establish their own righteousness, have not submitted themselves unto the righteousness of God" (Romans 9:1-3; 10:1-3).

From the Biblical references, it is a clear indication that passion had been identified as one of the great qualities of a successful soulwinner. The Lord Jesus Himself, the Great Soulwinner demonstrated this quality in His earthly ministry (Matthew 9:36). A believer with passion has a burning zeal that prompts him to travail until Christ is formed in sinners. He goes to sinners where they are in the house, in the market places, in the streets and in the neighbourhood. He goes with a sense of urgency because of the shortness of time and endlessness of eternity.

Soulwinning is a work of rescue! Rescuing souls on the way to perdition (Jude 23). Such work cannot be done with 'a cold feet.' We need burden and passion if we are to be fruitful soulwinners. The sobbing passion of Paul, no doubt, was the secret of his evangelistic fervor and fruitfulness. He declared, "I am a debtor both to the Greek and to the Barbarians." Owing debt is a burden! The effects of burden and passion are far-reaching which includes the following:

Intense and fervent intercessory prayers for the salvation of sinners (Exodus 32:32; Read Isaiah 53:12); Earnestness in evangelizing the unsaved (Isaiah 62:1); Deep burden, heaviness of heart, continual sorrow and unrelenting tears for the condition of the unsaved (Psalm 126:6; Read Isaiah 22:4 and Jeremiah 9:1); Commitment and consecration (John 9:4;1 Corinthians 9:16); Self-denial and unlimited sacrifice for the salvation of sinners (Esther 4:15-16); and Abandonment of personal gains, interest, leisure and satisfaction for the sake of souls (Philippians 3:7-8).

John R. Rice, author of 'The Soul Winner's Fire,' prayed, "May God give us tender, broken-hearts and weeping hearts as we go out to win souls." God is looking for better men than better methods. It is not great talents or great learning that God needs, but men, great in holiness, great in faith, great in love, great in fidelity, and great for God's service. The gospel should first be experienced and its power of salvation tasted before one is qualified to preach it to others, as no one can give to people what he didn't possessed.

Universality Of Soul Winning

The Great Commission is a God ordained ministry that calls every believer into preaching, spreading and proclaiming of the gospel of our Lord Jesus Christ (Matthew 28:18-20; 24:14).

Jesus commanded all His disciples to preach the gospel and disciple the nations. The command was to the generality of the disciples and contemporary believers all over the world. Therefore, the general and binding ministry of Christ's followers, preachers and ministers is soul winning and discipling or discipleship. The universality of the gospel also makes this ministry a universal one for all New Testament Kingdom workers and members. Whatever ministry anyone is involved in, he cannot be said to be pleasing God if he is not first involved in soul winning and discipling.

Preaching the gospel and teaching believers by following them up is a universal ministry for all. This is the Great Commission that the Lord has committed to all believers all over the world. It is not only the preaching of the gospel but also the discipling of converts that is binding on all believers and Christian leaders irrespective of any special area of ministry we are involved in. Whatever our calling is, we are to evangelize, and teach them (those born again) to observe all things whatsoever Christ has commanded - Whom we preach, warning every man, and teaching every man in all wisdom; that we may present every man perfect in Christ Jesus (Colossians 1:28).

The gospel message and its presentation were the greatest emphasis and focus of the Apostles in the Acts of the Apostle. Anywhere they went, whatever miracles they performed, they always climax everything with the message and teaching of the Word of God. They went, stood and speak all the words of this life in the temple to the people (Acts 5:20-21). Those chosen to serve tables preached the Word as well (Acts 6:5-6, 6-10; 8:4). The general ministry of all New Testament believers was the preaching of the gospel, they were people-centered in all they did.

The Genesis question of God to Cain was, 'Where is Abel thy brother?' (Genesis 4:9). The implication of this is that we are to be our brother's keeper and not just money keepers and instrument handlers and players alone. The king of Israel was too liberal to keep the man put or delivered into his hand; so he got the judgment (1 Kings 20:39-43). God has made all believers and leaders in the church watchmen over the souls of today's dying men, women, youth and children. Their blood will be required at our hands if we watch over materials and every other thing and fail to warn them, rescue them and keep watch over them (Ezekiel 3:17-21).

The Godhead's priority is the salvation of all men (2 Peter 3:9). The Father sent His Son save sinners (Luke 9:56; Revelation 22:17). Hence, any ministry we have that does not include this emphasis is not God-pleasing.

The Great White Throne Judgment requires that all believers and church leaders be involved in rescuing sinners and teaching the saints to avoid facing the judgment (Revelation 20:11-15; 2 Corinthians 5:11). Who are you persuading to avoid it and teaching to escape it today? These are the reasons all New Testament workers must have the universal ministry of preaching and teaching either through the pulpit ministry, church in the house (cell unit group) and on personal evangelism basis.

5

EFFECTIVE METHODS
OF SOULWINNING

T he fruit of the righteous is a tree of life; and he that winneth souls is wise" (Proverbs 11:30). Soul winning is leading a sinner to repent and wholly to God through Jesus Christ the Saviour. This is different from invitation, visitation and exhortation. For effectiveness, therefore, in soul winning, the believer needs the wisdom of God (James 1:5).

An effort to preach the gospel to the sinner should start with an effort to, first of all, understand him, his culture, religion, social and mental background. The soul winner should know his needs, concerns, ideals, doubts, fears in order to show him the way through to repentance and faith in Christ Jesus. As a soul winner, you will do well to know that Paul, Peter and Philip the evangelist are Bible examples of effective soulwinners. Jesus is the greatest soulwinner who ever lived. To effectively win souls, you should have divine commission, compassion and concern for the lost. You must avoid contention, acquire a good working knowledge of the Scriptures, be obedient to the voice of God and be persevering and persistent in prayer ((Acts 8:4-8, 26-27; Ezekiel 22:30; Galatians 6:9-10).

There are different methods of evangelism which are: Personal, Friendship, Mass, Door to door, Tracts and literature, Televangelism, Radio, Open-air preaching and internet/web evangelism. There are online gospel messages presented by using text, animation and video; but the most effective methods are personal and friendship evangelism.

Personal Evangelism

Personal evangelism, which is person to person witnessing for Christ, is deeply rooted in the Scripture with the aims of pointing the sinner to Christ. The sharing of the gospel on a person basis is God's strategy for effective completing of the Great Commission. It is an express command of the Scripture that calls for repentance. "Therefore they that were scattered abroad went everywhere preaching the word" (Acts 8:4). Jesus did it and we are to follow His example (1 Peter 2:21; Read John 4:21-31).

It is the purpose of the Pentecost and the standard practice of the Apostles (Mark 1:16; Acts 1:8; 8:1-4, 30-37). The Bible reveals that this is the primary purpose of our salvation. Jesus confirmed that, "Ye have not chosen me, but I have chosen you, and ordained you, that ye should go and bring forth fruit, and that your fruit should remain: that whatsoever ye shall ask of the Father in my name, he may give it you" John 15:16).

The possibilities of personal evangelism are boundless. The immense of personal evangelism is seen in the prophetic promises of Isaiah that a little one shall become a thousand and a small one a strong nation. In the world, it is said that a tree cannot make a forest. In terms of God's economy of spiritual multiplication, the fruitful tree can be counted for a forest. In terms of church growth and the filfilment of the Great Commission, the potential of personal evangelism are almost incredible. It can lead to exponential multiplication of converts and church members.

If a soulwinner wins a soul in a month and trains that soul to be a fervent soulwinner and both of them will repeat that process, each winning and training a soul per month, that missionary or soulwinner will have a membership of 4,096 in one year; and if two soulwinners earnestly repeat the above process, the result will be 8,192 members. Start with 50 Christians who love God and have zeal, faith and conviction and compassion. Let each of them win a soul per month. In 12 months, they will become 204,800 saved, strong and steadfast Christian soldiers for God.

Presently, if there was only one Christian in the world and he worked for a year and win a friend to Christ and if these two continued each year to win another and if every person in the world would be won for Christ. We need a fresh kindling of personal evangelism fire in our hearts (Matthew 9:36). Many hearts are cold or at best lukewarm. The passionate desire to see sinners saved is no longer a living experience of many Christians. The cares of this life, the rat-race for material acquisition and the "bless me" syndrome so common in contemporary Christianity choke the passion for souls. When our eyes are dry and our hearts are untouched by the destiny of unconverted; when our prayers are not saturated with strong groaning for sinners' salvation; when we shut our mouth from proclaiming the glad tiding, when daily, weekly, monthly and yearly soulwinning does not occupy any priority in our agenda, then we have fallen into lack of passion for the lost. The cry of our hearts must be, 'God give me souls or I die.'

Friendship Evangelism

There are many ways of presenting Jesus Christ to the sinful world (Proverbs 18:24; 1 Corinth 9:22-23, 27). Among these methods is friendship evangelism. It is a practical and realistic way by which we can lovingly and caringly share the gospel message with sinners. By this method, the soulwinner cultivates the friendship of the seeker with the aim of leading him to salvation and still keeps himself clear of his/her faults and vices.

One of the most effective tolls available to us for result-oriented friendship evangelism is **personal testimonies.** As effective as the tool is and as great as the toll is, it's still grossly neglected in soulwinning. Whereas our testimonies of salvation, God's mercies and cares over our lives, God's miraculous interventions in our life's problems, His protection over us and His provision will go a long way to minister to many who are finding things difficult and tough and to whom God seems far away.

Testimonies that will not only be effective and but also useful in soulwinning should not be void of personal experience but it must recount God's blessing (Psalm 66:16; Isaiah 63:7) and it must be short, straight-forward and inspiring. These should be personal testimonies of our unforgettable encounter with Christ, testimony of miracles and healings; and testimony of deliverance from satanic attack. The Samaritan woman employed this method and it was effective and successful (John 4:28-29, 39-40). This tool should not be neglected but be used efficiently with boldness and confidence. There are many characters in the Bible who, by their personal testimonies, inculcate great faith and courage into the life of the seekers. Remember that, the purpose of sharing our testimonies is to eventually lead such sinners to Christ and hence, a principle should be followed to be able to achieve our goal. We should pray to open up opportunities for the testimonies and prepare the hearts of the seekers (Colossians 4:2-24; Proverbs 16:1).

Wisely create an atmosphere of fellowship with the sinner or family to promote sharing together. Share your faith and do not share testimonies, back it up with the Word of God (Hebrews 4:12; Jeremiah 23:29). Also, live a holy life, an effective tool in the hand of a Holy God. In order to be a vessel unto honour, sanctified and meet for the Master's use and prepared unto every good work (2 Timothy 2:21). No matter how good or powerful the testimonies you share, it will not be effective unless they are shared with a holy life. Read Ezekiel 36:23. Be wise and tactful because the fruit of the righteous is a tree of life; and he who wins souls is wise (Proverbs 11:30). Friendship evangelism does not only entail the preaching of the gospel but it also involves willingness to impact souls. As we make up our mind to launch out afresh using testimonies to win souls for Christ, we must decide to very gladly spend until the prospect is won for Christ.

Mass Evangelism

Preaching the gospel to every creature requires the use of every evangelism method by the Church of Jesus Christ (Luke 5:17; John 6:2). One of such methods is mass evangelism or evangelical crusades that involve proclaiming the gospel to the crowd at the same time. In the Scriptures, we have the example of Elijah who gathered the whole of Israel on mount camel to decide on the true God. (1 Kings 18:17-24). Jonah proclaimed the message of God's love openly in the city of Nineveh (Jonah 3:4-10). Jesus Christ our Lord preached to the multitude on the mountain side (Matthew 5:12). Philip, in the city of Samaria, preached, Christ to the people (Acts 8:5-8).

Paul the Apostle, on the Mars Hill, declared the message of redemption to lost Athenians (Acts 17:22-23). These and many more were historical instances of crusade evangelism. In the recent past, ministers of God among whom are George Whitefield, D.L. Moody, C.G. Finney and Billy Graham to mention a few, reached hundreds of thousands through crusades. It is the method of making the gospel of Christ known to a great number of people gathered in a particular meeting point. This practice has been in existence from Bible days. Billy Graham in particular had held crusades in major cities of the world and that attracted millions of people. Reinhard Bonnke witnessed the conversion of more than 75 million souls throughout his over fifty years of conducting crusades. Therefore, a well-organized crusade is an avenue of meeting a large crowd of people with the gospel of Jesus. For a successful evangelistic campaign, there are basic principles in planning, understanding the purpose, knowing the people, determining the place and setting up of committee members. Preparation for a crusade should include: Prayer plan, publicity procedures, motivation and people's participation and preacher's preparation.

Finally, mass evangelism can be a power crusade (Acts 3:4-7;13:7), street meeting/evangelism, open air preaching in the market or parks, media outreach through radio, television, video, social media such as Facebook, general camp meeting using ideal avenues and Film shows for youth and children outreaches.

Internet Evangelism

Internet connectivity enables millions of souls all over the world to turn to the internet for their desperate need of answers to every challenge and question of each day. As the fastest and easiest growing communication media form in the history of the world, however, the message of salvation from sins can reach people that are far and near as long as they have internet access. Sharing the gospel online provides the opportunity for preachers to reach far more people than those in their geographic reach, most especially, in the regions that are difficult to evangelize. In this end time, the gospel messages can be generously launched as contributions to the websites for consumption by millions of browsers. It is very easy to swerve among online preachers, pastors, teachers of God's Word and counselors. Young converts in faith can be followed up, trained easily and discipled through the email, WhatsApp, Facebook or different online groups' correspondence of virtual congregations (Luke 14:22-23). Although, physical meetings are very significant but the physical building is not a necessity for people to come to know Jesus Christ as Lord and Saviour. Hence, the Internet today is a worldwide communication network that can facilitate effective Gospel communication and church growth.

6

SPIRITUAL WARFARE IN THE EVANGELISTIC MINISTRY

G ospel preachers, get ready for war. The Kingdom isn't a glass-toasting, apple-eating, all-comers jamboree. It is a place of eternal bliss in which entry is by fighting and winning wars. The Kingdom now suffers violence and only the violent gets into it and stays on in it until the Kingdom later comes. Until the final consummation of things when Christ's Kingdom is fully established and all the enemies of the Lord are crushed, judged and sentenced, there must be a war now! It is the will of God for all souls to be saved. The devil, the archenemy of God and man, is in the business of hindering men from salvation.

"But if our gospel be hid, it is hid to them that are lost: In whom the god of this world hath blinded the minds of them which believe not, lest the light of the glorious gospel of Christ, who is the image of God, should shine unto them ...For though we walk in the flesh, we do not war after the flesh: (For the weapons of our warfare are not carnal, but mighty through God to the pulling down of strong holds;) Casting down imaginations, and every high thing that exalteth itself against the knowledge of God, and bringing into captivity every thought to the obedience of Christ;...When a strong man armed keepeth his palace, his goods are in peace: But when a stronger than he shall come upon him, and overcome him, he taketh from him all his armour wherein he trusted, and divideth his spoils. He that is not with me is against me: and he that gathereth not with me scattereth" (2 Corinthians 4:3-4; 10:3-5; Luke 11:21-23).

Spiritual warfare is unseen and yet there is a real battle in the spiritual realm geared towards the rescue of souls of men and women who are held in satan's captivity. These captives comprise of various categories of sinners who are oppressed by satan and subjected to terrible afflictions and torments. Spiritual warfare is essential to pulling down the strongholds of satan and releasing those kept within his strongholds. In Luke 11:21-22, the Lord Jesus gave a vivid illustration of spiritual warfare.

Therefore, for a successful evangelistic outreach, spiritual warfare is of vital importance.

From ages past, the devil has been constantly waging war against all who belong to God (Isaiah 14:12-15; Ezekiel 28:1-19). A renowned writer described the devil as the evil one, the graduate in the School of deception and evil. True to this description, the devil deceived Eve in the Garden of Eden and caused Adam and Eve to sin against God. Subsequently, God decreed enmity between the serpent's seed and the seed of the woman (Genesis 3:1-19).

The devil incited David to count soldiers in Israel's army and thereby provoked God to wrath (1 Chronicles 21:1). He influenced Ananias and Sapphira to lie to God and this led to their untimely death (Acts 5:1-10). He instigated Peter to interrupt Jesus Christ when He (Jesus) spoke to His disciples about His death and resurrection (Matthew 16:21-23). Also, the temptation of Jesus is yet another proof of the devil's battle against God and His plan for mankind (Matthew 4:1-10). If the devil can war against Jesus, then he will pitch war against the believer. Even today, the devil is at war with the followers of Christ (2 Corinthians 10:3; 1 Timothy 1:18).

We may then wonder why there is this constant warfare. The Scripture clearly states it in John 10:10 that the thief comes to steal, to kill and to destroy but Jesus came that men might have life more abundantly. The devil is doomed for destruction and labour relentlessly to drag many people along with him into perdition. Hence, the reason for every believer to engage constantly in spiritual warfare in order to save souls into the Kingdom God.

In the book of 1 Thessalonians 2:18, Paul the Apostle declared that once and again, satan hindered them. Satan energized the ungodly to oppose God's will. He frequently attacks even believers by weakening their zeal for evangelism, putting fears into their minds and discouraging them when the results of evangelism are not realized immediately. Old Testament experiences of Moses and Pharaoh clearly illustrates the opposition of Satan.

The stubbornness of Pharaoh even after Moses and Aaron had performed many mighty signs and wonders also illustrates the extent the devil can go to keep souls in captivity. Instead of releasing the children of Israel, Pharaoh mobilized his magicians and sorcerers to oppose the power of God through Moses until they discovered that "this is the finger of God" (Exodus 7:8-13, 15-25; 8:1-32). This is why the Lord Jesus Christ confirmed that when a strong man armed keeps his palace his goods are at peace. The devil is this strong man and the souls of men are kept by him in his palace, using principalities, power, rulers of darkness of this world and wicked spirits in high places.

In like manner, the disciples who followed the Lord Jesus Christ soon realized that there are spiritual forces holding men in bondage as Philip encountered in Samaria where Simon the sorcerer held the whole city in captivity and Elymas also opposed Paul in Paphos on his missionary trip (Acts 8:8-11;13:4-13).

The Lord Jesus did not say that people will enter into the Kingdom of God with chuckles, looking pretty and tension-free. NO! The Lord says to strive to enter (Luke 13:24). Now, you don't strive except there's conflict, a barrier or an opposition. Doesn't that prove that a war is waiting for Kingdom seekers and Kingdom proclaimers? Satan and his formidable hosts are the aggressors and every mission effort that brings the gospel preacher face to face with the enemy triggers hostility. The preacher had better know this.

One reason some evangelization outreaches don't succeed is that the gospel preachers don't recognise (or refuse to recognize) the existence satanic hosts on guard at the vast prisons of human souls. Except these 'strong men' are bound and disarmed, soul-rescue will prove a huge joke (Matthew 12:29). That is the basis for warfare in gospel proclamation.

The gospel is the only means of freeing every soul of man from satan's perilous gulag. Satan's strongholds of captivity normally come tumbling down on impact with the tremendous power of the gospel. His iron gates are shattered and sinners are freed. Satan know this, he can't do anything to destroy the inherent power of the true gospel. So, he deploys all his arsenals and puts his armies on the red alert to prevent the gospel from sounding out.

The gospel magnifies Jesus and exposes satan as a captured crook on death-row. Satan is demystified and cut to size; his mask peeled off and exposed to the world for what and whom he really is - a dethroned, defrocked, dispossessed and defamed renegade (Isaiah 14:12-19; Matthew 28:18-19; Philippians 2:9-11); Colossians 2:15). Jesus is Lord! the gospel exclaims. Satan is a conquered, finished, fighting fool. You can see the reason for the war?

Satan may not want to easily accept defeat in his battle to possess human souls and let Jesus and His people rule in the New Heaven and New Earth, but he surely wants to rule here, now. He wants to be calling the shots and whipping everybody into line with sickness, disasters, heart-aches, poverty and untimely death. However, the gospel won't allow this to happen! The freedom Jesus offers affects both the body and soul and the very world of humans. For the power-thirsty Lucifer, this isn't a fair deal, so the war must go on!

Satan cannot change or repent because he has no second chance or opportunity. There is something in his devilry that will never make him recant, surrender and make peace with God. He can only fight on. Therefore, the gospel preacher shouldn't, at any time, expect a ceasefire and seek repose. Satan cannot be battle weary and the minister of the gospel had better hold firm the Sword of the Spirit.

Moreover, the glory that awaits all redeemed saints makes satan mad with envy. The saints are going to reign with Jesus in the Kingdom of God, the very privilege for which satan attempted to unseat God! Satan knows he cannot win this battle but he surely wishes to prevent as many people as possible from becoming saints and inheriting the Kingdom of God. Hence, the war!

Except the church of God awakes from their slumbering states of despondency and arise with the awesome power of Holy Ghost for the unfinished task of the Lord, souls of men will continue to languish in the stronghold of satan (1 Timothy 4:1-3; Read 2 Timothy 3:1-9).

Cults are on the increase all over the world today and holding man under the yoke of the strong man. This is the end-time mobilization effort of the devil to gather souls into hell fire; therefore, every soul-winner should be awakened to this realization in these Last Days and fight the battle for souls. Warfare, in its terms, is an aggressive or a violent conflict or continuous struggle between to opponents. In every warfare, there are usually the victors and the victims. The army with superior numerical strength, arms and ammunition, military strategy and higher morale always overruns the opposing force. The vanquished are victims who become prisoners and remain subjugated.

As it is in the physical, so also it is in the spiritual. The power of darkness is locked in grim battle against the power of light. As a result, believers are always in continuous warfare against the devil and his cohorts (Matthew 11:12). No believer in the battle field can afford to remain ignorant when the battle is fierce and the devil is armed with serious weapons to conquer, hinder soulwinning and destroy the believer. God, through Jesus Christ, has made adequate provision for every believer to be victorious in every spiritual warfare with effective weapons for a fruitful evangelistic ministry.

"Wherefore God also hath highly exalted him, and given him a name which is above every name: That at the name of Jesus every knee should bow, of things in heaven, and things in earth, and things under the earth; And that every tongue should confess that Jesus Christ is Lord, to the glory of God the Father...And they overcame him (devil) by the blood of the Lamb, and by the word of their testimony; and they loved not their lives unto the death" (Philippians 2:9-11;Revelation 12:11; Please read Ephesians 6:11-18).

The Godhead is not unaware of the demonic warfare waged against the souls of men and as such, He had made adequate provision for spiritual weapons that are effective in pulling down strongholds and releasing captives of sin and satan. Yet, the believer has to know the weapons and take the initiative to be on the offensive side of the warfare against devil, demons, barriers and attacks.

The weapons of our warfare are mighty through God in application to overthrowing all satanic arrangements and alliances. Possessing a thorough knowledge of what spiritual warfare demands and applying the weapons scripturally will help us reach all the souls held by the devil. When this is done, multitude of souls will experience the following:

Genuine salvation from sin, adequate knowledge of Christ's victory at the cross, purity of life (Acts 19:13-17), enduement of power and anointing through the Holy Ghost baptism (Acts 1:8; 1 Corinthians 2:4), power of God's Word (Ephesians 6:17), The name and the blood of Jesus (Mark 16:18; Revelation 12:11), dynamic faith in God (Mark 11:22-24), prevailing and persevering prayers (1 Thessalonians 5:17; James 5:16), discerning of spirits and yielding to the leading of the Spirit of God (Acts 16:6-10), passion and compassion for lost souls (Acts 9:36; Romans 10:11), and readiness to challenge and fight the battle until complete victory is won (2 Corinthians 10:6).

The Lord has commissioned the church to deliver the imprisoned souls through the leading and guidance of the Holy Spirit. He has given assurance of victory and the weapons. "Shall the prey be taken from the mighty, or the lawful captive delivered? But thus saith the Lord, Even the captives of the mighty shall be taken away, and the prey of the terrible shall be delivered: for I will contend with him that contendeth with thee, and I will save thy children ...The Spirit of the Lord is upon me, because he hath anointed me to preach the gospel to the poor; he hath sent me to heal the brokenhearted, to preach deliverance to the captives, and recovering of sight to the blind, to set at liberty them that are bruised, To preach the acceptable year of the Lord" (Isaiah 49:24-25; Luke 4:18-19).

The early disciples tried this and came back with results (Luke 10:17-19). Even the Church, after the ascension, continued in the same vein, had great results and we are bound to succeed if we all avail ourselves of all we are provided with in His Word. Therefore, we are well able to deliver the captives of satan by His grace. The prey of the mighty can be delivered and we can spoil the goods of the strongman.

Effective spiritual warfare will always produce a fruitful evangelistic ministry anywhere in the world. The Gospel releases great power through those who are skilled in spiritual warfare. So, a soulwinner or Christian worker who has faith in the name of Jesus and keeps the Word of God will pull down every stronghold of satan. This is the secret of divine breakthrough.

As we engage in spiritual warfare, we can have a successful evangelistic ministry in every city, village, province, state and community even where satan's seat is; and see multitudes troop into the Kingdom of God. "And the seventy returned again with joy, saying, Lord, even the devils are subject unto us through thy name. And he said unto them, I beheld Satan as lightning fall from heaven. Behold, I give unto you power to tread on serpents and scorpions, and over all the power of the enemy: and nothing shall by any means hurt you" (Luke 10:17-19).

What a joy it was, when Israel trooped out of Egypt and spoiled the Egyptians. What a great joy it was when the early disciples came back to the Lord and shared the testimonies of how they overcame the devil and his cohorts. What a great joy it was when Samaria was delivered from the yoke of Simon the sorcerer who have bewitched them for long time.

Likewise, if we acknowledge the relevance of warfare in missions and fight manfully onward, we will witness 'conversion explosion' of apostolic nature. We will fill Christ's Kingdom with souls of captives set free and nursed up into maturity. We can experience the same again if we are ready to pay the price and we shall experience it in Jesus' mighty name!

Binding The Strongman And Loosing The Captives

"Shall the prey be taken from the mighty, or the lawful captive delivered? But thus saith the Lord, Even the captives of the mighty shall be taken away, and the prey of the terrible shall be delivered: for I will contend with him that contendeth with thee, and I will save thy children. And I will give unto thee the keys of the kingdom of heaven: and whatsoever thou shalt bind on earth shall be bound in heaven: and whatsoever thou shalt loose on earth shall be loosed in heaven" (Isaiah 49:24-25; Matthew 16:19).

The fall of man in the Garden of Eden brought both individual and families under the yoke and servitude of satan. The devil is the strongman and the god of this world who took the advantage of the fall of man to keep him in bondage (2 Corinthians 4:4). Though God has promised to do the impossible by taking the prey from the mighty, yet He desires to work hand in hand with His children (believers) to fulfill His purpose on earth. But in ignorance, many believers live in perpetual fear rather than in constant victory.

It seems to them that perpetual victory over the enemy is a utopian experience realizable only when they get to Heaven. Yet, the consistent testimony of the Scripture is that God's original plan is for your complete dominion over the enemy and over your degree of captivity.

The Scripture is clear on the fact that the believers and God's children (household) can enjoy complete deliverance. To gain our deliverance and maintain perpetual victory in spiritual battle, God has given us the twofold strategy of binding and loosing. When we discover the divine plan for our lives and deploy the weapon of binding with all dimension of losing, we shall able to walk in perpetual victory. "And he increased his people greatly; and made them stronger than their enemies... Behold, I give unto you power to tread on serpents and scorpions, and over all the power of the enemy: and nothing shall by any means hurt you" Psalm 105:24; Luke 10:19). These verses of the Scriptures revealed that God's plan for us are greater than what we can possibly imagine.

Believers are created to be fruitful, to multiply, to have dominion and to subdue. We are to have dominion over the works of God's hand including the devil with all things under our feet. Crowned with honour and glory (Psalm 8:5), we are to bestride this side or eternity with divine authority, over the enemy. We can enjoy abundance from the father, be partakers of His divine nature and enjoy all things that pertain to life and Godliness (2 Peter 1:3-4).

Therefore, we can put the enemy where he belongs. "Thou madest him to have dominion over the works of thy hands; thou hast put all things under his feet...And the God of peace shall bruise Satan under your feet shortly. The grace of our Lord Jesus Christ be with you. Amen" (Psalm 8:6; Romans 16:20). This is God's plan for our life; this is what the enemy contends against (1 Peter 5:8).

One of the strategies of having perpetual victory is through binding. In relation to the church, Jesus guaranteed that whatsoever we bind on earth shall be bound in Heaven. To bind the devil does not imply tying him up so that he would not move forever; that will only happen during millennial reign of Christ according to Revelation 20:1-3.

To bind means to stagnate, polarize, to take captive, cage or imprison; to restrict or limit movement; to make hard for something to move, to cause something to obey you and to have controlling effect to fasten tightly as with bolt, screw or nut. The picture that emerges from above illustrations is that the believer can indeed exercise dominion or effect control over demons and demonic activities. You can limit, hinder, stop or restrict demonic influence over your life. If the devil is causing you any discomfort, it is because you allow him to do so.

In the name of Jesus, arise and bind the enemy and Heaven will seal your authority today! "The Spirit of the Lord Gᴏᴅ is upon me; because the Lord hath anointed me to preach good tidings unto the meek; he hath sent me to bind up the brokenhearted, to proclaim liberty to the captives, and the opening of the prison to them that are bound" (Isaiah 61:1). One thing about the binding and loosing strategies is that they must be practical. You can lose demonic hold upon your life, wife, husband, children, business, career and ministry.

To lose, therefore, implies to:
Free something from control – Luke 13:11, 16
Release from captivity – Isaiah 61:1
Untie – Luke 19:30; Zechariah 9:9
Discharge from prison – Acts 5:17-20; 12:10
Free from bondage or disease – John 5:5-9
Liberate from limitation or restriction – Acts 16:25-26.

In essence, God has made intercessory prayer a stirring summons to duty on the part of believers (Ezekiel 22:30). Intercession ushers enormous force that dispossesses the power of darkness of their captives or else, how can one enter into a strong man's house and spoil his goods, except he first binds the strong man? It is only then that he can spoil his house (Matthew 12:29). It also grants the assurance that we are not working alone but with the Owner of all souls, Who equally has promised His support in the battle for the souls of men.

Every battle to be fought requires planning and strategizing and spiritual warfare is not an exception. There is need to identify the lost (Romans 1:29-31; Revelation 21:8; Galatians 5:19-21). These are the religious, idolaters, the moralist, the worldly sinners and the backsliders. We are to discover the power working against their salvation (Ephesians 6:12) and pull down the strongholds of such powers; taking authority over them (2 Corinthians 10:4-5; Philippians 2:10-11).

It behoves us to plead with God to open the eyes of sinners to the salvation which is in Christ Jesus and remind God of His promises concerning the salvation of souls (1 John 1:9; 1 Timothy 2:3-4).

Now, when ministering deliverance to yourself or someone else, observe the following tested precautionary rules. They will help to boost the efficacy of the ministration and shield the minister from the dirt of counter-attack:

— Acknowledge the majesty and supremacy of the Trinity.
— Issue out commands with appropriate Scriptures.
— The seal of every command is Jesus' name. Demons don't obey any command except one issued in that name. But don't issue 'counter command.'
— Listen to the Holy Spirit for guidance as the ministration progresses.
— Let your mind be fixed on Christ and ignore all doubts.
— Avoid hollering and yelling. They are not necessary.
— Avoid laying of hands on the opposite sex wrongly. It may be very dangerous.
— Keep your eyes open to watch the goings-on.

— If the person makes a scene or the demon manifests, issue appropriate commands to deal with the problem and finish the demon off once and for all.

In Matthew 12:43-44, the Bible says "When the unclean spirit is gone out of a man, he walketh through dry places, seeking rest, and findeth none. Then he saith, I will return into my house from whence I came out; and when he is come, he findeth it empty, swept, and garnished." Demons are stubborn.

No matter how traumatic the wounds they sustained in a fight with Christians, they are sure to try to come back. Once the devil is bound with respect to a problem, we should ensure that he remains bound as regards that problem and once a man is loosed from demonic bondage, we should ensure that he remains ever free from that bondage. Once delivered, the devil can be kept permanently off by:

Purity of life – "We know that whosoever is born of God sinneth not; but he that is begotten of God keepeth himself, and that wicked one toucheth him not" (1 John 5:18).

Prayer - "Submit yourselves therefore to God. Resist the devil, and he will flee from you...Pray without ceasing" (James 4:7; 1 Thessalonians 5:17).

Permanent service for the Lord – "He suffered no man to do them wrong: yea, he reproved kings for their sakes; Saying, Touch not mine anointed, and do my prophets no harm (Psalm 105:14-15).

Proper attitude towards satanic emblems and practices – "Many of them also which used curious arts brought their books together, and burned them before all men: and they counted the price of them, and found it fifty thousand pieces of silver... Little children, keep yourselves from idols. Amen" (Acts 19:19; 1 John 5:21).

CHAPTER

7

CONSERVING AND DISCIPLING OF EVANGELISM FRUITS

The decision to follow Christ is the product of an evangelistic endeavour either by an individual of a church group. Fruitful evangelism that always leads to church planting where the fruits of evangelism are conserved and matured. Once decision is made for Christ by the seeker, the next step should be that of proper follow up aimed at conservation, maturation and multiplication of the fruit of evangelism. Like the sowing, watering and reaping of evangelism, follow up takes time. It is not an act but a process. There is no quick way to spiritual maturity and discipleship or Christlikeness. No other subject is more widely taught and illustrated in the epistles than personal, consistent, church-integrated follow-up aimed at leading the new converts from decision to true discipleship. Most of the epistle of Paul, Peter and John are follow-up letters to those new in the faith (Acts 15:36; 2:44-47).

To lead a convert from decision to discipleship requires personal contacts with the convert since such evangelism is just a channel by which the prospect is introduced to the soul winner. Christ was pre-eminently concerned with individual converts from the first day of decision to discipleship stage. He saw their needs of love, nourishment, protection, training and maturation. To achieve this goal of leading the new convert from decision to discipleship, the following steps are necessary and helpful.

Follow-up/Visitation

"Paul also and Barnabas continued in Antioch, teaching and preaching the word of the Lord, with many others also. And some days after Paul said unto Barnabas, Let us go again and visit our brethren in every city where we have preached the word of the Lord, and see how they do" (Acts 15:35-36). Follow up is an integral part of Biblical evangelism.

The result you get from evangelistic outreaches that are not coupled with detailed and intensive follow-up shows that is better not to plan a program than to have one without systematic follow up strategies. Much evil is done when a convert is not followed up. It is a picture of the convert drawn out of the sea of sin, satan and the world's system who then gets lost from the Church, a bane to the world and twice a child of hell. What a great loss! "And after he had spent some time there, he departed, and went over all the country of Galatia and Phrygia in order, strengthening all the disciples" (Acts 18:23).

Personal visit to the converts with the purpose of strengthening them is a method of bringing the new believer into maturity. The visit should be result-oriented and goal-centered. Coupled with prayers, the soul winner studies the Bible with the converts and shares tracts and Christian literature with them to foster growth and spiritual development.

Correspondence

Correspondence has been made easy through the use of mobile phones and internet connectivity such as text through WhatsApp, Facebook messenger and email and other social media platforms which are easy and fast ways to communicate with the new converts nowadays. Unlike early church, they make use of what is available to reach the unreached in gospel proclamation (2 Peter 3:1; 2 Corinthians 2:9).

Letters which were written under the influence of the Holy Spirit and sent out with fervent prayers have or carry maturing power for Christian converts. Some of the Apostles probably saw letters at that time as dependable assistants in their outreaches (letter can carry the message to places we couldn't reach). Over 75% of the New Testament are letters written to the believers to expound Christ-related history. Their messages were to instruct, warn, ascertain the believers' obedience and compliance, encourage and remind them of what they have learnt. (Acts 15:20-21; 1 Corinthians 4:14).

Integration

From the earliest time of the Christian faith, those who decide for the Lord are always integrated into the church through water baptism. Baptism therefore has been an integral part of Christianity. The three thousand converted at Pentecost were integrated into the church through baptism (Acts 2:38-41; 9:17-18).

Paul saw water baptism as a deed of transfer and an act whereby the baptized believer hands himself over to be the property or disciple of the one in whose name or authority he is baptized. The Scripture confirms that baptism is one of the foundation stones of Christian Faith. "One Lord, one faith, one baptism" (Ephesians 4:5; Read Acts 16:15; 19:5).

Conservation

Conservation is a process of preserving the faith and retaining the confidence of the new believer so that he does not yield to the temptation of sliding back into sin and the world. In other words, it is to serve as a family where the back door of backsliding is closed to whoever becomes a member (Acts 9:26-28).

This is an ideal situation where close personal relationship, interactions and fellowship exist and are developed amongst the brethren with the new members through apostolic teaching, corporate prayers and observance of the Lord's Supper (Acts 2:42-44).

Maturation

It is an arm of the church to bring believers to maturity in lifestyle, doctrine and ministry. "Therefore leaving the principles of the doctrine of Christ, let us go on unto perfection; not laying again the foundation of repentance from dead works, and of faith toward God... For the perfecting of the saints, for the work of the ministry, for the edifying of the body of Christ: Till we all come in the unity of the faith, and of the knowledge of the Son of God, unto a perfect man, unto the measure of the stature of the fullness of Christ" (Hebrews 6:1; Ephesians 4:12-13).

From the Scriptural references above, the duties of the ministers in the church of Jesus Christ are as follows:

Perfecting new converts and saints.
Involving the new converts in the work of the ministry.
Edifying the body of Christ with the new converts inclusive.
Unifying both the old and the new converts in faith.
Perfecting the Church in Christ life and ministry.
Bringing men to maturity in Christ Jesus.

Also, to mature new believers in Christ requires training both by teaching and by example. "Let no man despise thy youth; but be thou an example of the believers, in word, in conversation, in charity, in spirit, in faith, in purity. Till I come, give attendance to reading, to exhortation, to doctrine. Neglect not the gift that is in thee, which was given thee by prophecy, with the laying on of the hands of the presbytery... And the things that thou hast heard of me among many witnesses, the same commit thou to faithful men, who shall be able to teach others also" (1 Timothy 4:12-14; 2 Timothy 2:2).

Multiplication

"Praising God, and having favour with all the people. And the Lord added to the church daily such as should be saved" (Acts 2:47). Multiplication is simply applying the new law of reproduction in discipleship. Christ demonstrated the law of reproduction. Paul's ministry also stands as an example of the law of reproduction in a positive sense when he heaved a sigh calling on his little children, of whom he travailed in birth again until Christ be formed in them (Galatians 4:19).

Apostle Paul's desired reproduction and believed it applied not only to his doctrine but also his life style of soul-winning and discipling. He wanted men to live and think like Jesus Christ as well as know His goal of integrating, conserving and maturing new converts for discipleship all through his ministry.

Similarly, every leader should have his life ordered so that he might be able to reproduce the life of Christ in others. Also, leaders and co-workers should be like-minded. Workers should identify and agree with the leader's basis, goals and objectives in making the new believer the disciple of Christ (Mathew 28:19-20).

Submission to Water Baptism After Conversion
"Go ye therefore, and teach all nations, baptizing them in the name of the Father, and of the Son, and of the Holy Ghost Teaching them to observe all things whatsoever I have commanded you: and, lo, I am with you always, even unto the end of the world. Amen...He that believeth and is baptized shall be saved; but he that believeth not shall be damned" (Matthew 28:19;

Mark 16:16). It is very important to observe all things the Lord has commanded us in the gospel proclamation and water baptism.

After our reconciliation with God, the next thing to do is water baptism (Romans 6:3-4). Our Lord Jesus considered water baptism important as He did not begin His public ministry until He was baptized by John the Baptist (Matthew 3:13-17). Thereafter, He commenced His ministry and commanded His disciples to baptize those who believed the gospel as well. For every believer, water baptism is very important because:

It is the public declaration of our new identification with Christ.
It signifies our obedience to Christ's command.
It signifies our death, burial and resurrection to a new life with Christ.
It is a symbol of our true discipleship.
It shows our link with the Church, the body of Christ.

Summing this up, water baptism is Christ's command to those who have repented of their sins and come to faith with expression of their union with Christ in His death, burial and resurrection, through immersion in water in the name of the Father and the Son and the Holy Spirit which is the name of Jesus Christ. After this ordinance, however, the young converts are babies in the Lord; and as newborn babes, the desire for the sincere milk of the word is paramount to growth (1 Peter 2:2). These converts should be kept in the church and taught all those things which our Lord has commanded us.

CHAPTER

8

CHURCH IN THE HOUSE (CELL GROUP MEETING)

I t is the fundamental part of the church fellowship where members of the church in a neighbourhood fellowship, pray, worship and study the Bible together in an atmosphere of the home for closer relationship and care for one another (Acts 2:46-47; Read Exodus 18:13-23). It is a church within a church and a method of penetrating the neighbourhood with the message of Christ. It is an extension of church ministry and a church for the people among the people. The cell group fellowship, as a child of circumstance, has its root from the days of Moses in the Old Testament and was established in practice in the New Testament.

The principle underlining its establishment was drawn from Jethro's counsel to Moses to involve various levels of church leadership in the work of the ministry so as to solve the problem of the people. Therefore, cell group church or fellowship becomes necessary for proper care of the body of Christ, the survival of the ministries and the fulfilment of the calling of the church.

In the New Testament, Jesus preached the Word in the house (Luke 10:38-39). The use of houses as a place of fellowship and worship was practiced by our Lord Jesus Christ in His all-embracing ministry of healing, teaching, preaching, counselling and ministering to the needs of the people. He performed miracles and ministered deliverance to the oppressed and healing to the sick.

In Acts of the Apostles, there were references to the use of homes for breaking of bread, teaching, preaching, fellowship and praying (Acts 12:12; 20:20; Please read Romans 16:3-5; 1 Corinthians 16:19; Colossians 4:15).

Therefore, praise worship, thanksgiving, testimonies, prayers and intercession, teaching, counselling, and caring which characterizes the New Testament fellowship emanated from the practice of Christ and the early church.

A cell group has the potentiality of providing for the development of the whole body for the edifying of itself in love and making Christ's message of salvation to penetrate deeply into the fabrics of our neighbourhood and the community around. In the cell group fellowship, there's caring, edification, identification, fellowship and relationship, one, spiritual growth, preservation, multiplication, evangelism and ministry.

Leadership in the cell group is functional and active. The leader or cell group pastor is not just there to fill a vacancy; he's called to fulfill certain goals in the fellowship. He must lead by example not as being a lord over God's heritage, but being an example to the flock" (1 Peter 5:3). The leader should show example in:

Spiritual virtues and maturity (2 Peter 1:3-9).

Faithfulness. The cell group leader should show a good example in being faithful in small responsibilities, in commitment, handling finance and offerings, attendance to meetings and pre-meeting prayer times.

Humility and teachable spirit. "That which I see not teach thou me: if I have done iniquity, I will do no more...Let the word of Christ dwell in you richly in all wisdom; teaching and admonishing one another in psalms and hymns and spiritual songs, singing with grace in your hearts to the Lord" (Job 34:32; Colossians 3:16).

Enthusiasm and compassion for others. (Read John 2:17; Colossians 4:13).

Submission to leadership. "Likewise, ye younger, submit yourselves unto the elder. Yea, all of you be subject one to another, and be clothed with humility: for God resisteth the proud, and giveth grace to the humble" (1 Peter 5:5).

Personal appearance and balanced living. "Not purloining, but shewing all good fidelity; that they may adorn the doctrine of God our Saviour in all things" (Titus 2:10; Read 1 Peter 2:9).

In addition, the cell group leader is designated to help the people to function correctly and properly in the house and in the entire body of Christ. He is to ensure that those who are prone to wandering are kept within the confines of holy and righteous living. He must patiently confront the erring ones and labour to pull them back into the Kingdom.

He is to motivate them towards good works and excellence in Godly standards, and to help them to get and be God's best. The cell group leader is to help the members to learn all Christian principles of living and submission and to maintain Biblical order and control at all fellowship programs. He is expected to have a shepherd's heart as David who is tender, loving, caring and can abide as a faithful shepherd with the sheep always (Psalm 23:1-6).

Sacrificial lifestyle and commitment like Priscilla and Aquilla who could laid down their lives for the sake of others (Romans 16:3-5).

The cell group fellowship members are to comfort one another (1 Thessalonians 4:18); pray for one another (James 5:16); help, forbear and forgive one another (Ephesians 4:2,32); to make grudging one another an abominable thing (James 5:9); to make judging one another a total abhorrence (Romans 14:13); to love one another practically (1 Peter 1:22); to give room for hospitality (Romans 12:10); to help us serve one another (Galatians 5:13); to help us bear one another's burden (Galatians 6:1-2; Acts 20:35).

Moreover, it is to make us have compassion one for another (1 Peter 3:8); to promote oneness (Romans 12:16; 15:5); to discourage evil speaking (James 4:11); to foster cheerfulness and open greetings (romans

16:16; 1 Peter 5:14); to make backsliding a hard thing; to promote the growth and expansion of the body of believers; to guide and counsel; and to make the people live as salt and light - influencing the surrounding world by and large.

CHAPTER

9

CHILDREN AND
YOUTH MINISTRY

T he Lord Jesus has mandated the church to preach the gospel to every creature irrespective of age. Thus, as a whole, the church is to go out and reach sinners wherever they are – at home, on the streets, in the markets, school, stadia and everywhere. However, the church pays much attention to the souls of the adults than those of children. Yet God has graciously raised up children evangelists, teachers and pastors who have vision and mission for children evangelism.

Winning children for Christ is the act of preaching the gospel to them in order that they might be saved. When the Lord Jesus Christ was living the world, He commissioned all His disciples in Mark 16:15 to go into all the world and preach the gospel in every creature; every creature here includes the children.

The Lord surely has the children in His salvation program, for He said in Matthew 19:14 to allow little children and not forbid them to come unto Him for such is the Kingdom of Heaven. Thus, we should arise for the salvation of children.

"Rid me, and deliver me from the hand of strange children, whose mouth speaketh vanity, and their right hand is a right hand of falsehood: That our sons may be as plants grown up in their youth; that our daughters may be as corner stones, polished after the similitude of a palace...Let no man despise thy youth; but be thou an example of the believers, in word, in conversation, in charity, in spirit, in faith, in purity" (Psalm 144:11-12; 1Timothy 4:12).

Within the church, the Lord Jesus Christ has particularly given the children preachers and workers the task of preaching the gospel to children. Everywhere and anywhere they find children, it is mandatory to preach to them. They need to hear the preaching, believe and get converted by obeying the Word (Romans 10:14).

How then can we preach to them knowing full well that they are children and so, do not behave like adults. We need to adopt various ways that will make the gospel easily acceptable to them and with God's wisdom, we can win them for Christ. The use of various audio-visual aids materials such as pictures, drawings, paintings, charts, story-telling, wordless book, films stripes or tape recorders (Deuteronomy 6:4-9) is very effective with children of 3-5 years age-bracket. They will easily be interested and at the end of the exercise, they will give their lives to Christ.

However, teachers or children workers have to work hard to get these materials and use the appropriate ones at the right time. Age 6 to 15 years understand Bible passages; we should therefore, go to the Scriptures and preach the true gospel to them. Take them through the steps of salvation. Let them understand that they are sinners as the Scripture says in (Romans 3:23; 6:23). Tell them they need to know that they are part of all that have sinned by all bad things they do such as stealing, fighting, abusing others, being mean to others, telling lies to mention but a few. Tell them that despite their sins, Jesus loves them and died for them on the cross Calvary (Romans 5:6-11; 1 John 1:9).

Tell them to repent of all their sins and promise God they will not go back to them again (Acts 3:19). Ask them to invite Jesus Christ into their lives (Revelation

3:20). Ask them to believe that Jesus is in their hearts now (John 1:12). We can still use visual aids to support our preaching to these age groups. It will make them understand the gospel the more.

We should emphasize that Jesus can save them and He is the only one that saves. Now as children workers, we may employ different methods such as person-to-person evangelism, literature evangelism and friendship evangelism to spread the gospel. As we evangelize, we should be earnest, zealous and desperate.

We shouldn't carry on with the wrong notion that children still have so many years to live and shall be saved by and by. Death doesn't discriminate between the old and the young. Besides, the Lord may appear any time from now! After the children are converted, we still have to continue with the task in order to establish them in the faith. This we have to do by training them.

Generally, modern children and youth faces a lot of challenges which include crisis of transition; conflict of ideas and information; criticism from people and among peers, confusion of behaviours, carnality through peer influence; chronic sicknesses from bad habits and lifestyle and crossroads of indecision.

Worldwide values are being lost and youths have become the experimental tools in the hands of selfish alcohol brewers and cigarettes merchants; seductive fashion designers, satan-inspired musicians and film makers, among others. It thus becomes necessary that the children and youth ministry have a central place in the church today if we are going to fulfil the mandate of Christ and rescue these future leaders.

Positive Facts

Children and youth are potential leaders of tomorrow both in the church and in the society (Proverbs 14:34; 29:2; Read Daniel 3:28-30). Saved youth will give both the church and the nation a generation of righteous leaders.

They are great assets: bold, courageous and daring. "And the king spake unto Ashpenaz the master of his eunuchs, that he should bring certain of the children of Israel, and of the king's seed, and of the princes; Children in whom was no blemish, but well favoured, and skilful in all wisdom, and cunning in knowledge, and understanding science, and such as had ability in them to stand in the king's palace, and whom they might teach the learning and the tongue of the Chaldeans" (Daniel 1:3-4; Read 1 Samuel 17:33.37).

Children want acceptance, identification and a sense of belonging and will be committed to any cause. Genuinely saved at their youthful age, they stand and become agents of positive change (Psalm 144:12-15). They are hero worshippers and can easily be attracted to Christ as their hero. They are the link between their generation and the next one. They are malleable and could easily be motivated for God's glory. Also, they have great zeal for spiritual reproduction. Read John 1:40-46.

Negative Facts

Increase in technology: TV-video, internet activities, games et al have accelerated the rate of evils in the society and youth are the most vulnerable.

Moral vices: Hard drugs, shootings, immorality, bad peers, alcoholism and other menaces have contributed to the pollution of the mind of youths.

Wealth-craze: This has lured many a youth into robbery, prostitution, internet fraud to list but a few. The unconverted youth often become mighty weapons in the hands of the devil. Nevertheless, children and youth are on God's salvation agenda. The central purpose of children and youth ministry is to show the salvation and righteousness of the Lord to every generation.

The central purpose is to see the first century church ideals and convictions reproduced in the life of the twenty-first century youths. "My mouth shall shew forth thy righteousness and thy salvation all the day; for I know not the numbers thereof. I will go in the strength of the Lord God: I will make mention of thy righteousness, even of thine only. O God, thou hast taught me from my youth: and hitherto have I declared thy wondrous works. Now also when I am old and greyheaded, O God, forsake me not; until I have shewed thy strength unto this generation, and thy power to everyone that is to come" (Psalm 71:15-18).

Youth lusts: Lust is a strong desire to have something illegally, especially what you do not really need. It is evil passion, strong linking for sinful, mundane, self-gratifying things that cannot edify the soul.

"Flee also youthful lusts: but follow righteousness, faith, charity, peace, with them that call on the Lord out of a pure heart...Mortify therefore your members which are upon the earth; fornication, uncleanness, inordinate affection, evil concupiscence, and covetousness, which is idolatry" (2 Timothy 2:22; Colossians 3:5). Youthful lust is a leaven that spreads like wildfire among youths today and it comes in various shades:

Immorality: The most common youthful lusts involve sinful dating and immoral acts. This vice comes through inordinate affection for the opposite sex, watching obscene films, looking at pornographic pictures in the magazine, computers and on internet-ready phones; reading immoral novels, unhealthy attraction to same or opposite sex through careless dressing and undue closeness (Matthew 5:28).

Vanity: Pleasure seeking which makes young people uninterested in academic pursuits or crafts. It includes the time-wasting playing of computer, video and online games. It is inordinate ambition for wealth and fraudulent practices, fame and trying to be like an unGodly hero.

UnGodly Music and Dancing: Many churches even pattern their music after rock and funk in order to attract the youth to their assembly.

Dirty slang's and speeches: This they learn from colleagues in school, mates at joints or at play stations.

Juvenile Delinquency

There are some criminal, dangerous, weird and antisocial things youths do. Juvenile delinquency! The society is sitting on its time-bomb. With more than one half of the youth population living as delinquents who play religion and tag along sincere seekers of the Holy

God. What happens when the old saints go home? The delinquents take their place? God forbid! "Rid me, and deliver me from the hand of strange children, whose mouth speaketh vanity, and their right hand is a right hand of falsehood" (Psalm 144:11).

Youth ministers and church leaders should think deeply about the wave of juvenile delinquency and devise practical steps to stop or at least reduce the trend. That won't be possible if the case is not examined and the causes ascertained before cures are prescribed.

In the book of 2 Kings 2:23, some children mocked Prophet Elisha. Kindly read Ecclesiastes 11:9; 2 Samuel 13:1-2, 8, 11-14; 2 Timothy 2:22). These references show that juvenile delinquency is not a modern plague. It is dateless. The youth are inherently sinners. Adolescents are troubled by vanities, lusts and wild escapades.

The Adamic nature blossoms at childhood and sins, because of their novelty, are particularly attractive to probing minds and who can be more inquisitive than a healthy youth? Today, the list of juvenile delinquency is disquietingly long – vandalism, truancy, slothfulness, orgies, illicit sexual promiscuity, perversions, smoking, drug addiction, drunkenness, suggestive dressing, occultic association, hooliganism, stealing, robbery, violence, rape among other vices.

THE CAUSES OF JUVENILE DELINQUENCY (Romans 3:23; Psalm 51:4-6).

The Adamic nature: This is the inward depravity inherited from Adam and the reason the Bible declared all as sinners. It is the inner inbred sin of the carnal mind with physical and mental capacity of indwelling sin inherited from Adam. It manifests in the life of all human beings on earth who are not born again (Romans 5:12). This can only be changed through salvation.

Indulgence: The example of Eli and his children refers (1 Samuel 2:21-25). Despite the fact that Eli knew and was told about the misbehaviour of his children, he failed to discipline them. Also, Samuel (1 Samuel 8:3), despite the fact he was a prophet and a man of God without blemish, his children were wayward. He did little to change them. King David is another example (1 Kings 1:6) He did not rebuke Adonijah at any time.

Inability to discipline children when they do wrong (Proverbs 23:1; 22:15).
Influence of peer group (1 Kings 12:6-15).

Crooked behavioural psychology: Some argue that the youths will shape up as they grow up. They will stop the vices by reflex when they have been wizened and mellowed by age. How crooked!

Satan's systematic program: The devil recruits human rebels from among the youth population to fill the vacuum left by dead adults. All efforts to save the youth won't be successful as long as the devil is free to carry on with his recruitment. Moreover, the collapse of families and social dislocation contributed to juvenile delinquency.

In all these, the gospel of Christ is the cure for juvenile delinquency. It is the only source of transforming power. The youth won't change by learning behavioural drills. For such drill will lose their potency on impact with rock-hard human sinful nature. Only the gospel can blast sins off and free the human mind from where all vices proceed.

Now, how do we go about administering the gospel on the sin-laden delinquent? Get the delinquents. Be friendly and humble. Don't cast them as something exorcists eject, otherwise, they get angry and snub your gospel. Therefore, pray hard and preach Jesus.

Describe the problem of sin but point to the solution. Answer his questions if you can; otherwise, refer him to the church or a more experienced Christian minister or leader. Don't be frustrated if a delinquent doesn't accept the gospel at first attempt. Keep administering it on him. He will soon yield. The gospel is the power of God unto salvation.

The church at large should organize programs with youth appeal. Such a program should be preceded by tearing prayers of intercession and wide publicity. This is similar to mass evangelism. Let the atmosphere be tension-free but remember, you are not having a circus show. Preach the gospel. The message should be applied to juvenile delinquency.

It is important to point to the problems, show the fearful consequences and then, call the delinquents to repentance. Follow up should begin immediately after conversion. Some repentant delinquents may need rehabilitation. This is where formal counselling, government assistance and financial helps come in. Refer different cases to the church's youth section and follow them up.

Finally, let the former delinquents enlist as disciples. Give them the training but don't refer to them with their formal stigma. Juvenile delinquents! Look for them, pray for them and preach to them.

Characters Of A Youth Minister

Character refers to fruits or values; it is the hallmark of youth ministry because youths learn more by examples than precepts. In the midst of success-driven culture, it is important that the children and youth minister step aside to cultivate Christ-like character and conduct that will commend him to the hearts (not heads) of the youth. He should be a servant who shepherds young minds by his love and Godly example. He must be soundly converted, separated and purged from inward sins. He must be spirit-filled, resourceful, humble, teachable and responsive to Holy Spirit.

Although, a youth minister isn't a youth character and personality; he shouldn't be boyish in emotion, temperament, knowledge, wisdom and application of spiritual gifts. He must operate at a spiritual level higher than the youth if he will lead them from low level existence to high divine status that heaven demands of its citizens. He is called to lead, love, shepherd, disciple, mentor, counsel, equip and empower youths for character and influence, for victory and success, for life and ministry, for time and eternity (2 Timothy 4:5).

Vision For Neglected Children And Youth's Ministry

"And all thy children *shall be* taught of the LORD; and great *shall be* the peace of thy children" (Isaiah 54:13).

Every creature includes the children because the Lord surely has the children in His salvation plan. To catch the vision and develop it, the youth minister and soulwinner needs three motivators:

Compassion - Matthew 9:36-38
Love - 1 John 4:18-12, 20
Obedience - Mark 16:15; Matthew 21:28-30

Children are the heritage of the Lord. They are precious gifts from His throne. They are precious in His sight. The adults are nurses, guardians and builders of children. They are a people-group we are commanded to reach with the gospel. But soulwinning ministry among young people is a specialized mission field and the minister hoping to go into it must learn about its basics to avoid frustration and ensure success.

Youngsters aren't extensions of adults. They are independent beings with their own characteristics, sense of values, sensitivity and world-view. Though their process of conversion and discipleship may present a different pattern such that what goes in the harvest field may not hold in youth's and children's world. There is a common word used to describe most youth in the threshold of adulthood. It's the word teenager. This spells out the most peculiar characteristic of most youths, thus: Tender – still in their formative years and are so delicate.
Enthusiastic – full of exuberance, excitement and zest.
Emotional – could be touchy or friendly as the case may be.
Neither children nor adult – in-between people.

Adventurous – wants to try and test everything for hero worship.

Gullible – easily deceived and carried away; can believe anything.

Egocentric - self-centered.

Restless – full of energy (often misdirected).

These behavioural peculiarities reveal the reason children and youth could be easily won to either sides of spirituality. The commissioned servants of the Lord in the children church are called to renew their vision to their callings (Colossians 4:17). If we hunt them in the power of Holy Spirit, we will surely reach them before the devil arrives to lead them away into doom. The children and youth ministry have some peculiar problems, though (Ecclesiastes 11:9-10).

Young people's nature doesn't respond to the preachers' redemption quick fixes. Genuine transformation takes longer time than in adults and backsliding is common among them. For his constant exposure to the blitz of immorality, sensuality and obscenity on the internet, cell phone and the street and from peers; the youth find it hard to hold out after salvation unless the preacher can provide him with needed divine anchors.

Support is lacking for the children and youth ministers. Even in the church-based system, the department is less fed and funded being treated as necessary burden. No wonder, few people choose to be a children and youth worker in most churches. It's however, dangerous for the church to carry on as though her children and youth don't really count in God's reckoning. The church without a rich, strong and consistent youth spiritual development program has no future.

Only God can save souls; so, we have to intercede for the salvation of children and youths (Luke 8:15). Youth ministers should love young people and have compassion and pity for their vulnerability. Youths are attracted to ministers who have understanding of their tempting world and soft spot for their personality. While keeping his own maturity, a youth minister should identify with the taste and lifestyle of the youth to win their admiration.

There's also the principle of relevance. The content of the gospel message is the same for all men but its presentation, context and application vary with each people-group. The message meant for the youth should address their problems, apply to their aspirations and seek to clear their worries. Children and youth's gospel should be simple in content, graphic in details, rich in illustrations and catchy in delivery.

There are various methods by which the gospel may be presented to young people through literature distribution, film shows and weekend squash party. whichever methods or means the preacher employs, the essential thing is that it should be lively and of a short duration. It is good to know that no soul winning ministry can flourish if its converts are always lost as soon as they are won (John 15:16; 1 Peter 2:2).

Generally, the new born babe knows nothing. He's fully dependent on the parents for care, feeding, protection and training up until he reaches maturity. The same thing happens in spiritual parenting. Children are so helpless that the neglect of being well-nurtured, trained and protected from adverse conditions can lead to premature death, or can make the children victims of satanic manipulation. The Lord commands the youth leader to go and labour on until the new-born youth convert becomes a never-looking-back disciple. The conservation process begins with integration of the converts into regular fellowship according to Acts 2:41-42.

Natural parents keep a close contact with the children to guide, correct, counsel and set models of life style for them. They also set goals and plan for their expectations. Spiritual parents cannot do less. Plan must be made to help the youth and children converts at various developmental stages. They must be established in the faith through the teachings of some basic subjects such as Assurance of salvation (Romans 8:14-16) and Christian living (2 Corinthians 5:17; Ephesians 4:23-32).

Monitoring: We should serve as mentors for the children. Whatever we train them to do, we also should also do the same. Let them see Jesus in us. They should be able to see our good examples and follow suit (1 Timothy 4:12).

Quiet time: The child should be taught how to observe regular quiet time (Mark 1:35; 1 Peter 2:2). He should know that very early in the morning, he should wake up and go to a quiet place where he can talk to God in prayers and God can talk back to him through the Bible. He should have a jotter to jot down whatever the Lord speaks to him and he must pray to God to be able to do it.

Fellowship and integration: Teach the child and encourage him to attend fellowship with the household of faith. (Hebrews 10:14, 25).

Personal Bible study: We should teach the child and the youth on how to read his Bible daily (Joshua 1:8). You may buy a daily Bible reading guide for him and teach him how to use it.

Overcoming temptation: (Matthew 4:1-14) By enduring trials and persecution (Matthew 5:10-12), witnessing (Matthew 10:32; Mark 15:15) and by spiritual growth (2 Peter 3:18). As soon as the salvation of the children and youth converts is ascertained, he should be taught the importance of submitting to water baptism.

The teaching could be carried out at a formal converts' class or an informal home lesson depending on the number of converts. Whichever method is adopted, regular visits aimed at counselling, motivating, comforting and strengthening the convert in time of trials and persecution, are very essential.

The convert could move to other stages of discipleship namely delegation, supervision and evaluation as soon as he has mastered the foundations. Methods of training include instruction (Matthew 5:1-2), impartation (Luke 10:17-19), association, demonstration (Matthew 17:14-21) and delegation (Luke 10:1). Supervision comes in when the convert is assigned a work. Matured and trained converts should be enlisted in church-based ministerial church service. This is referred to as commission.

Preservation in children and youth ministry isn't an easy task. It calls for Pauline diligence, the patience of Job, the compassion of Jesus, the love of Christ and the minister's example of holy living. By God's grace, it can be done. The multiplication of false doctrines and teachers/prophets should stir up the children and youth minister or soul winner to double their efforts at purposeful follow-up for strategic growth of the new converts (2 Peter 2:1-3).

The objectives laid down should be consciously worked on to bring about steady spiritual growth. Godly strategies to help the children and youth stand firm in the faith and sound doctrine should be employed.

It should be understood that the young ones have a lot of potentials and seek the opportunities to be involved. The children and youth minister should closely watch over the converts to discover their gifts and talents to be able to enlist them in profitable service for the Master Jesus.

Finally, whatever effort or sacrifice we make these days to get the young ones converted, is not as important as labouring to see them established in sound doctrine to all fruitfulness (Titus 3:8). This is what purposeful follow-up is all about. It requires much time, effort and Godly determination.

The steadfastness and fruitfulness of our converts will prove whether we take follow-up seriously as much as we take evangelism.

10

THE GOSPEL MISSIONS

The Christian faith was born out of missions, spread by it and advanced through missions. The God we serve is a missionary God Who, over the years and ages, has been sending missionaries to the world. Jesus was sent from Heaven to the world. Jonah was sent to Nineveh and Paul to the gentiles. It's more than twenty centuries now that the son of God gave the command to church to evangelize the whole world (Matthew 18:19), yet the task of reaching the world with the gospel of Christ is still far from being complete.

Our Lord emphatically said, "And this gospel of the kingdom shall be preached in all the world for a witness unto all nations; and then shall the end come" (Matthew

24:14). It then becomes important that every assembly of believers endowed with both human and material resources should be involved in this great and serious assignment. Since Jesus is the Lord Who died for the sins of people of all nations, it is therefore mandatory for the church to carry the Gospel from the confines of the home missions across cultures, land and sea.

The challenges facing the church today concerning missions are manifold. There are challenges of unreached locations as it is clear from our Lord's command: "But ye shall receive power, after that the Holy Ghost is come upon you: and ye shall be witnesses unto me both in Jerusalem, and in all Judaea, and in Samaria, and unto the uttermost part of the earth" (Acts 1:8). According to the mission statistics of the traveling team of 2018 (http://www.thetravelingteam.org/stats), the world population is 7,68 billions, Total populations of unreached people is 3.14 billion. 'Most (97%) of the world's unreached people are located geographically in what some scholars call the 10/40 Window from West Africa across Asia between 10 degrees latitude north of the equator to 40 degrees north...2 Billion worldwide (all Catholic, Protestant, etc.) to make 28.6% of the world population, greater than 2% Evangelical Christian but still great numbers of unsaved'. The need of missionary outreach is most severe in the Middle East, Asia and

Eastern Europe where the average is one missionary to over 500,000 people because of severe persecution and martyrdom. Other challenges are those of ripened fields and open doors such as in the former Soviet Union regions. Without missions, those who sit in darkness will have no opportunity of seeing the light.

The Church of Christ needs vision for mission today like Apostle Paul in Acts 16:9-10, "And a vision appeared to Paul in the night; There stood a man of Macedonia, and prayed him, saying, Come over into Macedonia, and help us. And after he had seen the vision, immediately we endeavoured to go into Macedonia, assuredly gathering that the Lord had called us for to preach the gospel unto them." (Read Matthew 9:37).

The early church is a missionary church. They went everywhere preaching the gospel (Acts 8:4). Principal workers were sent out into the Gentile world. Now, should we sit in the pews and beckon sinners in?

The call to go into the world and preach the gospel to every creature remains ever fresh and binding. Therefore, the church and believers must rise up in spite of challenges posed by demonic strongholds of Christless religions. Despite the effort of the churches over the years, there are still innumerable multitudes that are within the stronghold of different religions and their traditions in the world today. The increasing wave of crime, drug addiction coupled with that of urbanization are major problems that confront the church today. Nominalism and worldliness of many Christian churches also call for aggressive missionary outreaches.

For effective missions, there's always commitment and consecration of the Christian workers. Consecration has been the bedrock of all missionary outreaches down the ages. The life of **Apostle Paul**, the missionary to the Gentiles, prominent missionaries such as **Adoniram Judson, William Carey, Hudson Taylor, Mary Slessor, David Brainerd** and a host of others, reveal that consecration is indispensable if the church and believers of today will succeed in missionary outreaches. Suffering of diverse kinds abound for all that would take Christ's Gospel to foreign lands.

For example, there could be satanic assaults. "And he shewed me Joshua the high priest standing before the angel of the Lord, and satan standing at his right hand to resist him...For we wrestle not against flesh and blood, but against principalities, against powers, against the rulers of the darkness of this world, against spiritual wickedness in high places" (Zechariah 3:1; Ephesians 6:12), as well as ecclesiastical suspicion (Acts 13:44-45, 50).

Religious leaders often view the missionary with suspicion. There could also be social contempt especially when the missionary could not speak the official language of the nation. The missionary may also suffer lack when funds become scarce as it often does (1 Corinthians 4:11-12). In spites of all these challenges, the missionary is never alone on the field. He has Christ with him (Matthew 28:20). His labour is also not in vain for there are great and exceeding rewards on earth and in Heaven for all Christ's labourers (Daniel 12:3).

Therefore, all lovers of Christ and His gospel should join Paul the Apostle in the statement of commitment to Christ's work. "But none of these things move me, neither count I my life dear unto myself, so that I might finish my course with joy, and the ministry, which I have received of the Lord Jesus, to testify the gospel of the grace of God" (Acts 20:24). The call is sounding loud and clear. Will you hear and forsake all to answer the Lord?

Principles Of Home And Foreign Missions
The challenge of the Great Commission is to take the whole Word to the whole world. When our Lord and Master gave the mandate to the early believers to go and preach the gospel, he did not set any geographical limitation nor any racial or language boundaries. The message of salvation is a universal gospel. "For God so

loved the world, that he gave his only begotten Son, that whosoever believeth in him should not perish, but have everlasting life.... And the gospel must first be published among all nations" (John 3:16; Mark 13:10).

The work of the church is not restricted to its immediate environs. It extends to "among all nations." Jesus died for the whole world and the gospel is for the Greek, the Jew, as well as the Barbarian. God wants every nation and culture reached. He expects converts from all the nations, kindreds, peoples and tongues (Revelations 7:9). The church should be a missionary either involved with home or foreign missions. The Christian faith is born out of missions, spread the through missions and advanced through missions.

A Church that relegates missions to the background is without doubt in the woods as regards what constitutes the whole counsel of God. "Therefore, they that were scattered abroad went everywhere preaching the word. Then Philip went down to the city of Samaria, and preached Christ unto them" (Acts 8:4-5).

Central to the ministry in the Bible is mission – a cross-cultural ministry to people in their own cultural and geographical settings. Mission is central to the charge of the Lord generally called the Great Commission. "And he said unto them, Go ye into all the world, and preach the gospel to every creature" (Mark 16:15). So, God expect to seek the lost both far and near.

The early church gives us good examples of effective missionary work – home and mission abroad. The church that will fulfill the Lord's mandate must adopt the principles, pattern and practice of soulwinning in the early church because:

Mission is the inevitable outcome of conversion (Matthew 4:19).

Every genuinely converted saint is a missionary of one kind or another (John 14:12).

Now, Christians should be assigned to the mission turf that they are ordained for Acts 13:1-2. While we must all preach everywhere, some are specially called to take Christ to specific places. Know your own turf by checking up with the Holy Spirit.

Every vision begins from home, the base of the Christian's conversion. No one may be sent abroad who haven't been proved at home. Home mission is the father of the foreign. "And that repentance and remission of sins should be preached in his name among all nations, beginning at Jerusalem" (Luke 24:47; Read Acts 1:8).

As a result, the need for a carefully planned and wisely executed mission program cannot be overemphasized.

There is need for comprehensive and vigorous missionary strategy in the church today. A good portion of church fund should be expended on missions. A church's vision for missions will determine its missionary burden and its missionary burden will determine its missionary budget. Christians who have been in their home countries all their lives may have to sacrifice leaving family, friends, acquaintances and bright prospects.

The church too may often be faced with the choice of either retaining workers who have proven ability and dependable personality in their home or headquarters church or sending them sacrificially to the mission field. Whatever is given for the cause of missionary outreach cannot be too costly. God had an only Son, yet He sent Him to the world as a missionary. Moreover, preparation for missionary work requires having a well-defined goal. Without goals the routines of life can become the result of life.

In addition to Christian experiences, the men and women who will bear the gospel to the ends of the earth should be people of deep commitment and persuasion. A rue missionary does not go to another land out of desire for adventure, travel, new experiences or just for the fun of it. In a sum, our preparation should include the following steps:

Survey/spy or map the field
Supplicate for the field
Strategize about the field
Supply funds for the field
Send the faithful to the field for harvest.

"And Paul chose Silas, and departed, being recommended by the brethren unto the grace of God. And he went through Syria and Cilicia, confirming the churches" (Acts 15:40-41). The Lord showed the early church that mission demands commitment. He sent principal workers or key leaders out on missions. Paul's call and commission portrayed a strong basis for missions. Right from his conversion, the Lord indisputably directed his mission to the conversion of the gentiles (Acts 9:15; 26:16-17).

Peter the apostle, one of the pillars of the early church, also had a missionary call. Though he exclusively spent his life and ministry amongst the Jews, the Lord appeared to him in a vision and directed him to the Gentile community of Caesarea, the house of Cornelius. The early church devoted their lives to both home and foreign missions. They all preached everywhere they went (Acts 8:4; 11:19-21). Their foreign missionaries consisted of scattered disciples (Acts 8:4); Soul-winning deacons (Acts 8:5), specially called and commissioned disciples (Acts 14:1-4), serving professionals and tentmakers like Luke the physicians and Aquila's family. These missionaries returned and gave detailed reports to the mission coordinating centers (Acts 14:21-28; 18:22).

They were well equipped, supported by the home church, characterized by large-heartedness, emotional stability and freedom from racial prejudice. They were adaptable, networking as teams and wisely integrated cultural differences into the dynamics of the gospel (Acts 15:1-32; 1 Corinthians 9:19-23). They explored unreachable lands and established a trail of churches which they strengthened through constant visit, epistles, delegates, intercessions, teaching and choosing formidable indigenous leadership (Acts 16:36; 14:24-25; 20:17-35; 18:19-20).

They followed the leading of the Holy Spirit, planned their outreaches, stayed long in thriving lands and left when compelled to do so, but allowed others on the work (Acts 13:49-51). Mission isn't picnic. The missionary, whether at home or abroad, isn't on a relaxation sight-seeing trip; he has a business that allows no indulgent fun, demands self-denial, calls for consecration and commitment and puts the flesh to death.

Our Saviour Jesus Christ expects every living member of His body to spend for the salvation of men. He commands us to join Him in His efforts in seeking the lost sheep scattered all over the world. If He gave His life for us on the cross, what can we do for his delight?

Laity Involvement In Church Planting

Church planting resulting in church growth should be the desire of every preacher and pastor. This, however, depends on the leader himself and the presence of an effective laity. The pastor, no matter the level of his power, wisdom or anointing, still needs the people.

A leader that craftily resists the gifts of other leaders or members in the involvement of church growth and development have skeleton in his cupboard and a case to answer in the court of heaven. "Curse ye Meroz, said the angel of the Lord, curse ye bitterly the inhabitants thereof; because they came not to the help of the Lord, to the help of the Lord against the mighty" (Judges 5:23).

Solomon might be a man of great wisdom, but he, nevertheless, needed the challenge and counsel of others. David might be a man after God's heart, a musician and skillful warrior in battle, but he still needs direction from the Holy Spirit to appoint a choir master and form a team of warrior leaders. While the pastor reaches the congregation, the congregation reaches the society. "And Jesus, walking by the sea of Galilee, saw two brethren, Simon called Peter, and Andrew his brother, casting a net into the sea: for they were fishers. And he saith unto them, Follow me, and I will make you fishers of men" (Matthew 4:18-19)

Since no preacher or pastor can single-handedly fulfill the Great Commission, the laity who are set in the body must be motivated, mobilized and involved in church planting works (Ephesians 4:16). By all standards, the work of church planting is great and expensive.

The people to be reached are various and numerous, and to ensure great success, effective coverage and proper execution, everyone in the church should be involved as the pastor carries them along the path of church planting. "Now he that planteth and he that watereth are one: and every man shall receive his own reward according to his own labour. For we are labourers together with God: ye are God's husbandry, ye are God's building" (1 Corinthians 3:8-9).

The laity are the members in the local church as distinct from the clergy. The laity constitutes the vast majority of church members. They may be educated or uneducated and are of various vocations. This is the company of the redeemed people in the local church. They have fulfilled the following conditions: repentance and faith in Christ, forgiveness and peace with God, love of God and the brethren without reservation, total obedience of God's unchanging word, submission to leadership and desire for faithful service in the local church.

These people cannot be in the church doing nothing; for the Lord has a purpose of bringing them into the church and they are to be involved in church planting activities. No matter how great the pastor's ability, talent, wisdom, he needs the laity as labourers in the vast harvest fields. "Pray ye therefore the Lord of the harvest, that he will send forth labourers into his harvest" (Matthew 9:38).

The church leader has a great task of gradually making all his church to become active fishers of men through the grace of God. Developing the laity involves training and mobilization. The laity should be taught, trained and exposed to the work.

Training could be formal or informal, general or specialized as instructed by God's Word. "And the things that thou hast heard of me among many witnesses, the same commit thou to faithful men, who shall be able to teach others also" (2 Timothy 2:2). The type of training could be for general members (Acts 14:22) or workers and there should be constant evaluation, feedback, re-planning of strategies among leaders in the church (Acts 20:17-21), and training on prayer, intercession and counselling.

It is very important the leader (pastor) needs to master various techniques to ensure members and workers of the church keep learning and developing through role playing, discussion and conference procedure, lecture and case study (Luke 8:9; 10:1; Acts 1:1-3).

Another thing the pastor needs to take into consideration is mobilization - the act of placing workers (trained laity) on the work. As people come into the church and get cleansed and transformed by the Lord; they are trained and put in the work force for the benefit of the body of believers. (2 Samuel 20:23-26; Acts 13:1-3). The pastor of the local church can interview the trained workers to determine their suitability, competence, availability for effective service and place people in areas that their abilities fit. Effective development of the laity leads to availability of workers (teachers, evangelists, prophets, pastors, choristers, ushers and children workers) for church planting.

Church planting is the result of evangelism (Matthew 28:18-19). Every evangelical outreach should aim at producing disciples that will remain in the faith and in the church. The conservation of the fruits forms a greater part of the Commission which must be given proper consideration. The commission of Christ to the church is to preach the gospel and make disciples of all nations.

When we gather all these converts together in a particular locality for the purpose of perfecting the work of redemption in their lives through constant teaching and training either directly or indirectly, we are said to be planting churches. Consequently, we should be set for the developed and trained laity in the church for church planting. Not all the laity will become church planters. However, a church planter must be a man or woman of God.

Urban Church Planting

Urban church planting simply means the establishment of churches in urban areas to cater for converts that of evangelism thrusts. Establishing churches in such areas helps to preserve the converts and create better forum fort converts' growth. It also brings the church closer to the people and makes ground for more evangelism and impacts positively on the community. "The churches of Asia salute you. Aquila and Priscilla salute you much in the Lord, with the church that is in their house" (1 Corinthians 16:19). The need to plant churches in our urban cities appears great because of the peculiarities of urban areas and towns, which demand urgent and serious evangelistic efforts. These include the following:

High concentration of sinners in cities and towns.
High rate of social vices such as prostitution criminal activities, drug addiction, gang killings, shooting and killings, manslaughters, sexual assaults, robbery, homicides, street boys and girls. The remedy to such vices rests on the gospel of our Lord Jesus Christ, hence, the need to plant churches in those areas.

Moreover, our urban cities are home to modern-day cults operating in the name of money-making activities. Wresting such people from the hands of the evil people demands that they are evangelized and churches planted to cater for them.

In the New Testament, churches were planted in cities like Ephesus, Rome, Philippi, Jerusalem, Colosse, Corinth, Antioch, Samaria to mention but a few through the efforts of apostles and disciples. It was from these cities that the gospel eventually spread to the hinterlands.

"Now they which were scattered abroad upon the persecution that arose about Stephen travelled as far as Phenice, and Cyprus, and Antioch, preaching the word to none but unto the Jews only. And some of them were men of Cyprus and Cyrene, which, when they were come to Antioch, spake unto the Grecians, preaching the Lord Jesus. And the hand of the Lord was with them: and a great number believed, and turned unto the Lord" (Acts 11:19-21).

The success and sustainability of any church planting strategy in the urban centers require – prayers, planning, sacrifice and wisdom in conservation of the results of evangelistic program and in removing barriers that keep men out of God's Kingdom. Under the guidance of the Holy Spirit, appropriate methods and strategies are essential to the success of church planting. The two common examples are:
Personal evangelism and Mass evangelism.

Any of the two above could be used; but a survey may be necessary to determine which is most appropriate. The method to be adopted depends on the location and leading of the Holy Spirit. After the souls have been won through any of the program, efforts should be made to conserve the fruits of the outreach by organizing follow-up activities. Thereafter, the new converts are baptized and integrated into the church.

Through church planting especially in the urban centers, the Kingdom of God experiences both numerical and spiritual growth. It has been said that the most effective way of conserving the fruits of the gospel is to open a local church for the converts in places close to where they live. The task of evangelism is not complete until even local churches are established. In turn, these churches will multiply in membership giving birth to daughter churches which also mature and give birth. So, the cycle continues.

CHAPTER

11

PENETRATING RESISTANT AREAS WITH THE GOSPEL

B ut if our gospel be hid, it is hid to them that are lost: In whom the god of this world hath blinded the minds of them which believe not, lest the light of the glorious gospel of Christ, who is the image of God, should shine unto them...Ask of me, and I shall give thee the heathen for thine inheritance, and the uttermost parts of the earth for thy possession...All the ends of the world shall remember and turn unto the LORD: and all the kindreds of the nations shall worship before thee. For the kingdom is the Lord's: and he is the governor among the nations...And all flesh shall see the salvation of God" (2 Corinthians 4:3-4; Psalm 2:8; 22:27-28; Luke 3:6).

Gospel resistant areas, nations, cities, towns, villages and communities are hostile to the missionary and his gospel message. In some places, there's legislation against inter-religious conversion, antagonistic religious sect, hostile audience, uncivilized, rural people group. They repel every effort to reach them with Christ and prefer darkness to the light that the gospel brings.

The whole world is full of darkness (evil). The Bible even describes it as "...this present evil world (Galatians 1:4) that lieth in wickedness (1 John 5:19) whose god is satan. The Bible says he is the "power of darkness" (Colossians 1:13) the enemy of God and the arch enemy of man.

Satan is not a mere "evil power," "influence," or the "negation of good," but an intelligent spiritual personality, ruler of a vast kingdom, and god of this world who rules through personality, power, rulers of darkness of this world (thrones) and spiritual wickedness in high places (a host of demons, evil spirits).

These demons, evils spirits, and human agents (witches, wizards, necromancers, herbalists, diviners, magicians, sorcerers and false prophets are satan's tools, who engage in a ceaseless warfare against believers and God's work on earth. "Who opposeth and exalteth himself above all that is called God, or that is worshipped; so that he as God sitteth in the temple of God, shewing himself that he is God" (2 Thessalonians 2:4).

All continents of this world have such resistant areas; and missionaries are wary of going there as satan and his cohorts always aggressively and actively antagonizing the ministry of Jesus Christ. Yet, in spite of resistance and the existence of such dark places on earth, the Lord's command to preach the gospel everywhere to all the people must be obeyed. The Lord does not exclude any place on the earth globe from His outreach list; which means an area's resistance is not permanent.

There's no easy way to gospel proclamation, satan would always put up a resistance as we attempt to snatch his captives from his stronghold. The strongholds of satan are the bulwarks of fortresses built by the devil against his prey to keep them in perpetual bondage and slavery. He uses his evil devices to make such a captive of sin, sickness, oppressions, oppositions, defeat, failure, bondage, sorrow et al. In order to achieve his diabolical intentions, he has a tight network of organized demonic spirits with specialized areas of evil activities; but if it is addressed with the divine weapons given to us by God, there will be victory.

The light of God will shine to penetrate the dark place. "For we wrestle not against flesh and blood, but against principalities, against powers, against the rulers of the darkness of this world, against spiritual wickedness in high places... And the light shineth in darkness; and the darkness comprehended it not" (Ephesians 6:10-12; John 1:5).

The area will buckle and give in to the preacher's message if we're available for the Lord. "And I sought for a man among them, that should make up the hedge, and stand in the gap before me for the land, that I should not destroy it: but I found none. Therefore, have I poured out mine indignation upon them; I have consumed them with the fire of my wrath: their own way have I recompensed upon their heads, saith the Lord God (Ezekiel 22:30-31).

There are some organized powers and forces that oppose the penetration of the gospel in some areas. Some of these causes range from spiritual to man-made and physical problems. The following are some of the reasons some people groups, nations and communities may be resistant to the gospel message:

Satan's machinery (2 Corinthians 4:3-4), Saint's mistakes (Galatians 2:11-14), Location and origin (Acts 16:19-24), Organized persecution (Acts 4:18; 5:40), Dearth of selfless prayer (Ezekiel 22:30-31), Religion, social, political factors (Acts 21:27-32) and activities of false preachers (Matthew 7:15). Satan always relishes his habit of keeping his captives in perpetual bondage. He is the catalyst behind every resistance the missionaries encounter on the mission field as they strive to make sure that people are liberated from sin to serve God in holiness. In such area, however, there may be:

Prohibition of preaching: Prohibition of gospel materials and church-based fellowship.

Legislation against inter-religious conversion (John 9:19-22).

Religious fanaticism/bigotry: "And Saul, yet breathing out threatening and slaughter against the disciples of the Lord, went unto the high priest, And desired of him letters to Damascus to the synagogues, that if he found any of this way, whether they were men or women, he might bring them bound unto Jerusalem" (Acts 9:1-2).

Idol worship and the seat of satan location: "I know thy works, and where thou dwellest, even where Satan's seat is: and thou holdest fast my name, and hast not denied my faith, even in those days wherein Antipas was my faithful martyr, who was slain among you, where Satan dwelleth" (Revelation 2:13; Read Daniel 3:1-7).

Dictatorial government and suppressive laws: The persecution of Christians almost always involves violence and thousands of Christians have been imprisoned. Many converts to Christianity in these areas mostly face abuse and violence for their decision to follow Christ. Some have been attacked, sexually assaulted, detained and killed for their faith. (Daniel 6:1-9).

Ideology of man that brings division: From the political points of view, an ideology among the people within the communities may create more differences. Ideologies such as capitalism, conservatism, communism, fascism, feminism, pacifism, socialism and environmentalism, to mention but a few, create more barriers to the proclamation of the gospel of Christ in many areas. (Read Acts 17:18-21).

Predominant spiritual powers: "But there was a certain man, called Simon, which beforetime in the same city used sorcery, and bewitched the people of Samaria, giving out that himself was some great one: To whom they all gave heed, from the least to the greatest, saying, This man is the great power of God. And to him they had regard, because that of long time he had bewitched them with sorceries" (Acts 8:9-11).

There are territorial spirits as in the case of the prince of the kingdom of Persia which hindered the prayers of saints like Daniel's prayers for twenty-one days (Daniel 10:12-13). It could be a persistent activity of demonic spirits designed to weaken one's hand and slow down the progress of Church planting, evangelization and mission work just like Sanballat and Tobiah stood against Nehemiah (Nehemiah 4:1-3).

The opposition of Bar Jesus during Paul's ministration to Sergius Paulus was a stronghold that could have hindered his salvation if Paul had not taken authority over him. "Then Saul, (who also is called Paul,) filled with the Holy Ghost, set his eyes on him. And said, O full of all subtilty and all mischief, thou child of the devil, thou enemy of all righteousness, wilt thou not cease to pervert the right ways of the Lord?" (Acts 13:9-10).

It could be likened to a wall of barrier hindering the penetration of the gospel in certain communities, cities or nations just as Jericho wall that was straightly shut up because of the children of Israel so that none went out and none came in (Joshua 6:1; Numbers 13:19).

Keys To Gospel-Resistant Areas

Above all, the Lord is still saying, "Ask of me, and I shall give thee the heathen for thine inheritance, and the uttermost parts of the earth for thy possession" (Psalm 2:8). When the Lord gave the Church the Great Commission, He knew that we will encounter some difficulties but He gave us the keys that unlock every door or barrier to the preaching of the gospel (Matthew 16:18-19; 18:18-20). God's decision on demonic strongholds is that they should be destroyed. He has also provided adequate and mighty weapons for their destructions.

The knowledge of these weapons will give power and effect in prayers for the destruction of strongholds that oppose the Gospel of our Lord Jesus Christ. Nothing is impossible with God if we rightly employ the weapons of:

God's Word: "For the word of God is quick, and powerful, and sharper than any twoedged sword, piercing even to the dividing asunder of soul and spirit, and of the joints and marrow, and is a discerner of the thoughts and intents of the heart" (Hebrews 4:12; Read Jeremiah 5:14; 23:29).

God's word is the Sword of the Spirit. It has penetrating power to cast down and probe into the realm of unseen forces. It is the hammer that breaks satan's walls of fortifications if rightly used and applied in sustainable prayers (Psalm 2:8; Acts 4:23-31).

The Victory of the Cross: "Blotting out the handwriting of ordinances that was against us, which was contrary to us, and took it out of the way, nailing it to his cross;

And having spoiled principalities and powers, he made a shew of them openly, triumphing over them in it (Colossians 2:14-15; Read 1 John 3:8; Ephesians 1:19-21).

The Name of Jesus: (Philippians 2:5-11; Mark 16:17-18). The name of Jesus is above all names. God has highly exalted Him and given Him a name above every name. Jesus has also given us authority to cast out demons in His name. All strongholds of opposing forces can be cast down and out in the name of Jesus.

The Blood of Jesus: "And they overcame him by the blood of the Lamb, and by the word of their testimony; and they loved not their lives unto the death" (Revelation 12:11; Read Exodus 12:13). The Blood of Jesus is eternal with Father God's DNA. And there is great power in the Blood of Jesus! The blood of the Lamb was a sign of victory for the children of Israel. Much more is the blood of Jesus Christ powerfully efficacious over the strongholds of the devil, for the believer.

The Anointing of the Holy Spirit: "And it shall come to pass in that day, that his burden shall be taken away from off thy shoulder, and his yoke from off thy neck, and the yoke shall be destroyed because of the anointing... How God anointed Jesus of Nazareth with the Holy Ghost and with power: who went about doing good, and healing all that were oppressed of the devil; for God was with him. Isaiah 10:27; Acts 10:38; Read Zechariah 4:6; Isaiah 59:19). It is the anointing that breaks the yoke. The Spirit of God created all things and nothing created can withstand the power of its Maker.

Prevailing Prayers: No Christian can pray effectively except he is strong in the Lord and in the power of His might; and is living a consistent victorious life that is Spirit-filled. God has set us apart as His battle axes and weapons of warfare that cannot fail (Jeremiah 1:10; 51:20).

To pray in prayer is to be determined, resolute and importunate until the answer is secured and the closed doors are opened; and yokes are broken (1 Kings 18:41-45). It's to be like the widow, who will not give up until the unjust judge avenged her of her adversary (Luke 18:1-8). Actually, God is still standing and waiting to avenge for all those who will cry unto Him in prevailing prayers.

Jacob prayed prevailing prayers to overcome Esau, his life-long rival (Genesis 32:24-28); Hannah prayed it to secure a Samuel from God (1 Samuel 1:12-18); Nehemiah prayed to ensure the continuity of the rebuilding of the Wall of Jerusalem (Nehemiah 1:4, 4:9); Daniel prayed with fasting to receive a message for the captives Israelites in Babylon (Daniel 9:3; 10:12-14); the early church prayed to enforce the release of Peter from Herod's stronghold (Acts 12:5,7); Paul and Silas prayed to break the chains and open the prison doors (Acts 16:25-27) and the Syrophoenician woman prayed to obtain the deliverance of her daughter (Matthew 15:21-28).

Prevailing prayers include worship, thanksgiving, supplications, intercessions, binding and loosing; and praises. It can also be strengthened and made effectual with fasting because "...this kind goeth not out but by prayer and fasting" (Matthew 17:21).

Sometimes, it is the prayer of praises that will cause an earthquake to destroy satan's hold of oppression and opposition forces, like the shout of praises brought down the Wall of Jericho and caused every man bound to be loosed in the prison when Paul and Silas sang praises unto God (Psalms 149:6-9; Acts 16:25-27).

Put on the whole armour of God and use the God-given weapons in prevailing prayers and all the strongholds of opposing forces will be pulled down. Believers are the battle axes of the Lord. Arise!

Faith: It is good to know that our faith must be demonstrated and put into action by engaging in profitable programs that would expand the Kingdom of God such as:

Spy program/spiritual mapping (Numbers 13:1-3; Joshua 2:1).

Signs and wonders (John 4:48; Mark 16:17-18).

Subtle, systematic outreach (1 Corinthians 9:22).

Special services, supply of basic needs like foods, clothing, educational and medical assistance. With the Saviour on our side, our victory is sure in Jesus mighty name.

The 10/40 Window (Gospel Resistance Area)

This is the resistance belt and the home of the largest unreached people in the world. It encloses 69 nations above Asia, middle east and North Africa. The area is stubborn and opposes the propagation of the gospel with billions of people in captive by rulers in authority, and with all sort of demonic manipulations, deceptions and undue influences of perpetual bondage.

The area is Biblical and historical significance with four of the world's dominant religious blocs that saturated with Buddhism, Hinduism, Islam and non-religious (atheists) sects, and numerous spiritual strongholds. "But if our gospel be hid, it is hid to them that are lost: In whom the god of this world hath blinded the minds of them which believe not, lest the light of the glorious gospel of Christ, who is the image of God, should shine unto them" (2 Corinthians 4:3-4).

The majority of the world terrorists' organizations are based in the 10/40 window. There are over 85 percent people remaining unevangelized and never having the opportunity to hear and respond to the Gospel of Christ.

The 10/40 window in the world map stretches from 10 degrees to 40 degrees of the equator with approximately 66 percent of the world's population. This is the home to the majority of the world's poorest of the poor, more than eight out of ten live in the 10/40 window.

Since it is entrenched in the stronghold of satan, the Kingdom of God has not fully penetrated this area. But according to John 1:5; the Bible declared, "And the light shineth in darkness; and the darkness comprehended it not."

In view of this, believers need to rise up and pray and pull down all demonic strongholds, subdue kingdoms and rulers of darkness, principalities and powers that hold the people captives for the gospel light to shine and penetrate for the salvation of souls.

Also, it behoves us to pray that God should send more labourers into His vineyard, protect all missionaries and Christians in this region with divine help of open heaven, courage to continue in boldness and power of witnessing.

Above all, all Christians around the world should awake in corporate prayers daily for the lost, the groups of people, governments and leaders in the 10/40 window (joshuaproject.net).

12

FAITHFULNESS IN SERVICE AND REWARDS FOR THE FAITHFUL PREACHERS

F or the kingdom of heaven is as a man travelling into a far country, who called his own servants, and delivered unto them his goods. And unto one he gave five talents, to another two, and to another one; to every man according to his several abilities; and straightway took his journey...Moreover it is required in stewards, that a man be found faithful" (Matthew 25:14-15; 1 Corinthians 4:2).

In the Kingdom's work, there are Scriptural conditions for acceptable service. God looks beyond service to see the servant's life. There should be perfect love for

God and man (Deuteronomy 30:6). A life of humility, obedience to God and His words, love, integrity in all matters, lifestyle of holiness, endurance, separation from worldliness and submission, become easy.

He pursues God's business with fervency and faithfulness. This is because works of the ministry without works of righteousness portend great earthly and eternal dangers to the preacher as well as the flock. Fingers are not equal and it is not a mistake; that is exactly how God created them. But each functions in its own capacity - faithfully doing its own part.

There are diversities of spiritual gifts and ministries in the household of faith. The Spirit of the Lord writing through Apostle Paul said, "For the body is not one member, but many... But now hath God set the members every one of them in the body, as it hath pleased him" (1 Corinthians 12:14, 18). Whatever works you are doing for the Lord, whether small or great, the Lord expects you to be faithful.

Faithfulness is all that the Lord requires of you even when the duty doesn't suit your fancy or rhyme with your social status or spiritual standing. For the Lord won't accept any excuse for failure. "But the Lord said unto him, Go thy way: for he is a chosen vessel unto me, to bear my name before the Gentiles, and kings, and the children of Israel" (Acts 9:15).

There is a clarion call for faithful, committed and dependable ministers in God's vineyard. God is daily searching for men and women, young and old who are ready to serve Him selflessly, committedly and faithfully. Unfortunately, many of those who take up appointments in God's house are only after material and financial benefits they could acquire by serving the Master. But a faithful servant does whatsoever his hands find to do with all his might, knowledge and wisdom (Ecclesiastes 9:10).

He does not tolerate sin or seek self-glory or reward from men. He is undeterred by affliction, persecution, want and initial failure. He holds fast that which the Lord has given him and labours on in hope. He daily trims his lamp of service with oil of faith, purifies his heart of all doubts and ensures that his hands are continually on the plough (Luke 9:62).

Our Lord Jesus was faithful to His Father who sent Him and He remained faithful up until the end. Obedience to God and His Word characterized His life and ministry and He's our perfect Example in all things. As servants, preachers or ministers, we are called to follow His steps as:

Being able men. That is, being saved, sanctified and Spirit-filled (2Timothy 2:19-21).

Fearing God. Doing all that we do as before God (2 Corinthians 4:1-2).

Loving the truth of the Word of God (John 8:31-32).

Hating covetousness (Hebrews 13:5-6).

Being of good report within and without (Acts 6:1-3; 1 Timothy 3:12-13).

Always abiding in Christ (John 15:1-8; 1 John 3:5-6).

Being in humbleness of heart and meekness of Spirit (2 Timothy 2:24-26). Faithfulness glues the believer to his duty post. It moves him to the task assigned to him rain or sunshine. Faithfulness is tenacity of conviction and consecration to purpose and practice. The faithful does not waver, cringe, or recant. He remains unmovable in his conviction, firm in his confession, fixed in his commitment and consecration and is ready to die at his duty post.

The reason many ministers fail in their service to God is their lack of faithfulness. Those who doubt the power of God or are unwilling to pay the price rather look for help in Egypt using diabolical powers to deceive the unguided flock, yet saying, "Thus says the Lord" when the Lord has not spoken. They are unfaithful.

If your convictions, commitment and consecration change with the time and tide of prosperity and popularity, you are unfaithful. Whatever work you are doing for the Lord, whether small or great, recognized or otherwise, faithfulness is required by God. Therefore, God expects you to be faithful. To do this, you need to:

Magnify your office and put your best into it (Romans 11:13).

Discharge your duties with a high sense of responsibility (2 Corinthians 2:16).

Be bold, uncompromising, forthright and unsparing in the denunciation of evil and declaration of the truth (Acts 4:13; Titus 1:13).

Adhere to the Biblical standard and to God who has called you (2 Corinthians 4:2).

Live a challenging true Christian life (Matthew 5:16).

Be determined to please the Lord, not surrendering to people's whims and caprices. Faithfulness compels you to stick to your confession of faith (Romans 6:1-2), conviction as regards to Biblical truth (Titus 1:7-9), consecration to the performance of your own part of the Great Commission, church perfection at all costs (Hebrews 11:13-15) and commitment to the preaching of the word, teaching, maturing and pastoring the converts and perfecting the saints (Acts 6:2,4; 8:1,4:5:14-42).

"With all lowliness and meekness, with longsuffering, forbearing one another in love" (Ephesians 4:2). These virtues or graces are to characterize believers at all times.

"**...With all lowliness.**" This speaks about humility. There is a great price on lowliness and humility in the Bible. "Better it is to be of humble spirit with the lowly, than to divide the spoil with the proud" (Proverbs 16:19). God gives more grace to the humble to live a lowly life, devoid of pride and conceit. In dealing with others, believers and preachers are to deal justly and show mercy and compassion as well as walk humbly before God. The grace of lowliness is not restricted to some, but it is for all to be clothed with humility.

"**...With all meekness.**" This is the very character and nature of Jesus. "Take my yoke upon you, and learn of me; for I am meek and lowly in heart: and ye shall find rest unto your souls" (Matthew 11:29). Christ is to be our Pattern and Model in life, if we are to walk the worthy life.

"**...With long suffering.**" Part of the preacher's worthy walk is to manifest and demonstrate longsuffering without complaining. It embodies patience and endurance.

"In your patience possess ye your souls." (Luke 21:19). There is the possibility of losing the grace of God, His blessings and our souls because of impatience. We need to be patient after we have done the will of God, so that we can receive the promise of God.

"...Forbearing one another in love." Love is what makes a child of God different from other people. Offences will come, but we are not to give room to bitterness, wrath, anger and malice but be "kind one to another, tender-hearted, forgiving one another, even as God for Christ sake hath forgiven you" (Ephesians 4:32).

To please God, we must allow the Spirit of God to produce these virtues in our lives. The more they abound, the more our lives and services in the Kingdom will be pleasing unto the Lord.

However, when God's work is not done in God's way, it can't get God's results with consequences in the life of such a steward. "Cursed be he that doeth the work of the LORD deceitfully...And that servant, which knew his lord's will, and prepared not *himself*, neither did according to his will, shall be beaten with many *stripes*" (Jeremiah 48:10; Luke 12:47).

There are inherent dangers in living below Scriptural standards as ministers of God. God is mocked. By Him, thought and actions are weighed. Only those who live above board will receive rewards. Blemish will bar anyone from entering Heaven or receiving reward for work done. "Not everyone that saith unto me, Lord, Lord, shall enter into the kingdom of heaven; but he that doeth the will of my Father which is in heaven. Many will say to me in that day, Lord, Lord, have we not prophesied in thy name? and in thy name have cast out devils? and in thy name done many wonderful works? And then will I profess unto them, I never knew you: depart from me, ye that work iniquity" (Matthew 7:21-23).

Preaching and ministering and messing up will make the Word to be of no effect in the lives of hearers; those outside the flock will be discouraged from coming in and the real church growth may be impossible. Formalism will set in and the presence and power of God is withdrawn. Devil will be free to wreak undisclosed havoc among the membership. True revival becomes an uncommon occurrence. The experiences of ministers or leaders in the church of the living God who despised the call unto holy living serve as warnings for all today.

Balaam lost his prophetic office because of covetousness. He despised contentment that Godliness brings and was lost forever "Which have forsaken the right way, and are gone astray, following the way of Balaam the son of Bosor, who loved the wages of unrighteousness; But was rebuked for his iniquity: the dumb ass speaking with man's voice forbad the madness of the prophet" (2 Peter 2:15-16).

Korah, Dathan and Abiram had the problem of pride, self-will and rebellion; they were men of renown - famous in the congregation (Numbers 16:1-3). Their fame and privilege got into their head and they lost their heart to satanic manipulations. They lost everything – position, privilege, preaching, property and posterity (family). Wilful disobedience to the revealed Word of God was the undoing of the children of Eli, **Hophni and Phinehas** (1 Samuel 2:12-17).

Alexander, Hymenaeus and Philetus were classical example of false doctrine, heresies and blasphemy. "Of whom is Hymenaeus and Alexander; whom I have delivered unto Satan, that they may learn not to blaspheme...And their word will eat as doth a canker: of whom is Hymenaeus and Philetus; Who concerning the truth have erred, saying that the resurrection is past already; and overthrow the faith of some" (1 Timothy 1:20; 2 Timothy 2:17-18).

Demas loved the world (its gold, glamor, girls, and glory) and forsook God "For Demas hath forsaken me, having loved this present world, and is departed unto

Thessalonica; Crescens to Galatia, Titus unto Dalmatia "(2 Timothy 4:10). The world and holiness don't rhyme and there is no Biblical evidence the Demas got to Heaven. Therefore, let us beware!

Judas Iscariot got his salvation directly from our Lord Jesus Christ and had a great position among the apostles, but the love for riches turned him into a betrayer (Please read Matthew 26:14-16, 47-50; 27:3-5). He lost his bishopric and his salvation forever. As an apostle, he went to hell. Jesus said, "You cannot serve God and mammon (the god of money).

Samson had power but without purity. He was a man anointed from his mother's womb but immorality made him a sport for enemies. He became blind and died prematurely in enemies' camp (Judges 16:1, 21-25, 30).

Solomon had wisdom and many gifts but outlandish women turned his heart from true God. Many preachers today have become mere spiritual pieces of bread because of infidelity, immorality and uncleanness. "Did not Solomon king of Israel sin by these things? yet among many nations was there no king like him, who was beloved of his God, and God made him king over all Israel: nevertheless, even him did outlandish women cause to sin" (Nehemiah 13:26). There was no record that he repented and made it to Heaven.

Strange fire led to the untimely death of **Nadab and Abihu**, a loss of further usefulness and a taste of hotness of hell fire on earth (Leviticus 10:1-3). When a preacher begins to raise up a church and minister in unscriptural manners, or bringing extra-biblical practices into ministry, such a preacher is going Nadab's and Abihu's way!

Holiness of life is not optional; it is the will of God for all Christians. We must resolve to seek, secure, sustain daily and live holiness-saturated lives. Remember that, "...the foundation of God standeth sure, having this seal, The Lord knoweth them that are his. And, let everyone that nameth the name of Christ depart from iniquity. But in a great house there are not only vessels of gold and of silver, but also of wood and of earth; and some to honour, and some to dishonour. If a man therefore purge himself from these, he shall be a vessel unto honour, sanctified, and meet for the master's use, and prepared unto every good work" (2 Timothy 2:19-21).

Moreover, through the neglect of personal fellowship by being busy here and there, many have allowed their anointing to dry or become stale and the fire is quenched. Once we failed to allowed the presence of the Lord to rub on us through personal fellowship, we lose everything: for without me ye can do nothing"

(John 15:5). Paul told Timothy, "But thou, o man of God, flee these things, follow after righteousness…, fight the good fight of faith" (1 Timothy 6: 11-12).

God has appointed us to succeed in ministry. He wants us to bring forth fruits that will abide. True ministerial success is not in fame, popularity, financial breakthrough, beautiful gigantic edifice, large congregations (full of carnality); but in abiding fruit, holy and Heaven-minded believers ready for the rapture or prepared and determined to die in Christ if He tarries. If we fail (God forbid), it is because we have failed to lay hold on His grace and to employ His promises and provisions since He has made available unto us "all that pertain unto life and godliness." What then are the means, helpers or channels of success in divine ministry?

Life changing encounter with Christ (2 Corinthians 5:17). Separation and life of holiness (2 Corinthians 6:14-18). Clear conscience (Acts 24:16). Power of the Holy Spirit (Acts 1:8; Luke 24:49). Divine presence (Haggai 2:4). Faith for success in ministry (Hebrews 11:6; Mark 11:24). Consistent and rich personal fellowship with God (1 Peter 2:2). Life of prayer and intercession (Luke 18:1; 1 Thessalonians 5:17).

Faithfulness in service (1 Corinthians 4:1-2).

Zeal for souls to be saved (Romans 1:16; 1 Corinthians 9:16).

Continuous aspirations for greater exploits (Philippians 3:10, 14).

Making Our Calling And Election Sure

"Wherefore the rather, brethren, give diligence to make your calling and election sure: for if ye do these things, ye shall never fall: For so an entrance shall be ministered unto you abundantly into the everlasting kingdom of our Lord and Saviour Jesus Christ. Wherefore I will not be negligent to put you always in remembrance of these things, though ye know them, and be established in the present truth" (2 Peter 1:1-12). This passage of the Scripture highlights the responsibility of Christians, especially preachers and workers so as to ensure that their position in Christ accomplishes its divine purpose.

The nature of our calling does not allow for passivity. We have to work with God faithfully with all the grace He has given us to justify His unquantifiable investments in us by our walk and work. God never fails to do His own part, and we shouldn't fail to do ours. We have to "give all diligence to make (our) calling and election sure." The language is clear. True and fruitful Christianity is no picnic. Working for God carries a price tag. It costs to serve the

Master (Matthew 11:29; Luke 9:23-26). If we endure the pain and shame that go with our calling then we "shall never fall." God says, "...an entrance shall be ministered unto you abundantly into the everlasting kingdom of our Lord and Saviour Jesus Christ" (2 Peter 1:11).

But if we are careless about our calling and election; if we fail to tame the flesh, feed the soul, flee from sin and serve the Lord without conditions, then we repudiate the grace that saved us, nullify our salvation and sign up for God's wrath (Matthew 25:24-28,30). God forbid that in Jesus name – Amen!

Our calling and election into the Kingdom of God is a mystery. Fellow Christian soldiers, we do not merit the call and the commission that follows it. Most of us are not of the stock of Abraham. Our ancestors wined and dined with devils, worshipped idols and lived in sin and were born in transgression. We didn't know the way of peace and purity; we groped daily in darkness.

Looking back and weighing our past in the balances of God's Word, we should be overwhelmed with the shame of being so vile and crooked creatures (Romans 6:20-21). But thanks be to God. "The people which sat in darkness saw great light; and to them which sat in the region and shadow of death light is spring up" (Matthew 4:16). We should appreciate and jealously guard our calling and election in view of its greatness and uniqueness. We should ensure that we fulfil its purpose and do nothing to rubbish it.

For it is: (a) A high calling of God (Philippians 3:14); (b) Heavenly calling (Hebrews 3:1); (c) Holy calling (2 Timothy 1:9; 1 Peter 2:9); (d) Hopeful calling (Ephesians 2:4); (e) Humble calling (1 Corinthians 1:26-31; Acts 4:13); (f) Irreversible calling – in purpose and practice (1 Corinthians 7:20-22,24; Romans 11:29); (g) A call unto liberty from bonds of sin (Galatians 5:13); (h) A glorious call (1 Peter 5:10); (i) A call unto suffering for the Kingdom's sake (1 Peter 2:13-15,16-24); (j) A call unto blessing (1 Peter 3:9); (k) A call unto service (Matthew 4:19; Titus 2:14; Romans 12:4-8; Ephesians 4:11-14); and lastly but foremost, it is a call by God (1 Peter 2:9). Thus, our calling is incomparable.

We dare not trade it off for a mess of the world's pottage. Having come from Heaven, our calling and election are not subject to men's interpretation and value judgment. God by Christ called and ordained us; and He is the only Judge Who weighs our actions. His approval is only what matters in all our ministerial activities. We do nothing to merit this call. Thus, we stand in awe before God and "pass the time of (our) sojourning here in fear" (of sinning) - 1 Peter 1:17.

We are humble, holding on tenaciously to the operations of our calling. We are ever found at our beat, ever ready to serve, "fervent in spirit, serving the Lord." We dare not recant or cringe though the heathen rage and the devil rave. Our mind is fixed. We delight in the spiritual glory that attends our calling now and relish in advance the splendor of excellence that awaits us beyond the crystal shore. Yes, we may suffer for daring to be different. But we labour on, rejoicing in the hope of our calling that assures us of painless, deathless, blissful and prosperous eternity.

Even on earth, our calling and election guarantee all-round blessings; and we seek how to share these blessings with the world's people in the honour and proclamation of our Lord Jesus Christ. What a call! How great, marvellous and mysterious!! Praise the Lord!!!

On one hand, our calling and election, however, attract various challenges. The devil is angry with us because we left his camp and enlisted in the Lord's army. He is at war with us and we have to fight to repel his forces and hold our position. "Finally, my brethren, be strong in the Lord, and in the power of his might. Put on the whole armour of God, that ye may be able to stand against the wiles of the devil. For we wrestle not against flesh and blood, but against principalities, against powers, against the rulers of the darkness of this world, against spiritual wickedness in high places" (Ephesians 6:10-12; Read 1 Peter 5:5-9).

On the other hand, we are faced with the task of spreading the gospel light to all world's people who sit in darkness and are bound in sin and trespasses; and those ruled by the devil who are oblivious of the fact a Saviour has died to redeem their souls. Unless we face these challenges and overcome them, our calling and election will end in failure.

We are called and elected to serve the Lord (John 15:16). Our service is to preach the Word, show forth Christ's glory and power and make disciples of all nations and people. The task of evangelization and souls' maturation is greater now than ever. We have to justify our calling and election by making all our efforts to sending out the gospel, mature converts and raise churches. There is work for every servant of Christ to do. We are not to be Christian workers in name only.

We should be Christian workers in deeds. If you are not doing anything in the Master's vineyard, you will be numbered among the unprofitable servants and be marked for eternal banishment to hell (Matthew 25:22-27, 30; John 15:2).

Our services, however, demand unconditional commitment and consecration. Nothing should separate us from the love and service of Christ. Not even marital crises, unemployment, poverty, sicknesses and persecutions (Romans 8:35-39). We should be ready to die doing God's will, if need be.

Moreover, our calling and election requires perfecting. This means we need to make all the coverts better, surer, stronger and more Christ- honouring and we do this by using certain additives of faith. "And beside this, giving all diligence, add to your faith virtue; and to virtue knowledge; And to knowledge temperance; and to temperance patience; and to patience godliness; And to godliness brotherly kindness; and to brotherly kindness charity. For if these things be in you, and abound, they make you that ye shall neither be barren nor unfruitful in the knowledge of our Lord Jesus Christ. But he that lacketh these things is blind, and cannot see afar off, and hath forgotten that he was purged from his old sins" (2 Peter 1:5-9).

We should check up the totality of our calling and identify which additives are missing and then add them. Doing this takes diligence, study, prayer and practice. We must be ready to give all it takes to perfect our calling and election.

The process of perfection leads to growth and we have to ensure that we grow in our calling. For God has purposed that that our calling and election should be dynamic in nature. We are programmed to grow in grace, holiness, ministerial assignments; to grow in the knowledge of God, grow in power and wisdom for service. Grow in all aspects of spirituality. Always remember that we are tempted to look back, deny the faith and follow the world. Hence, there is need for our continuity in our calling and election.

The forces of sin and satan and life's troubles and conflicts sometimes appear to be too powerful for our faith and resistance. At such times of trial and temptation, however, we should turn to the Lord, His Word and the Holy Spirit for strength and comfort. We should look up and gaze forward to the glory that awaits us. We should pray hard and remember the saints that have gone before us. We should remember that the Lord cares for us and we are not alone in life's storms.

We should remember Lot's wife and move on. We dare not become careless with what was given to us by Christ's death. To preserve our calling, we need to walk worthy of it (Ephesians 4:1, 17-32; 1 Peter 2:11-12); Shun the world (Romans 12:1-2); Mind heavenly things (Colossians 3:1-4); Be vigilant, watchful and stable about Bible doctrines (1 Timothy 4:16); Watch, pray and work (Matthew 26:41); Endure afflictions and avoid compromise (2 Timothy 4:5); and look unto Jesus during trials and temptations (Hebrews 12:2-5).

Our calling and election have glorious eternal consequences. If we cherish and keep to our calling and election and we face the challenges and overcome them by God's grace, how great and manifold shall be our gains! Righteousness pays. Working for God attracts great dividends. On earth, we enjoy the Lord's protection, preservation, prosperity and power. We see the fruits of our labour and rejoice that we are partners with God in the task of changing destinies. We hinder the devil's army from holding people captive and deliver the 'preys of the terrible.' Finally, in Heaven, oh, we shall receive glorious crowns and live happily forever with our blessed Lord!

Incredible Crowning Of The Faithful Stewards
*"And, behold, **I come quickly; and my reward is with me, to give every man according as his work shall be.** I am Alpha and Omega, the beginning and the end, the first and the last. Blessed are they that do his commandments, that they may have right to the tree of life, and may enter in through the gates into the city...Therefore, my beloved brethren, be ye **stedfast, unmoveable, always abounding in the work of the Lord,** forasmuch as ye know*

that your labour is not in vain in the Lord... His lord said unto him, Well done, good and faithful servant; thou hast been faithful over a few things, I will make thee ruler over many things: enter thou into the joy of thy lord" (Revelation 22:12-14; 1 Corinthians 15:58; Matthew 25:23).

From the above Scriptures, Christ wants us to be committed to what He has assigned us to do and if we are faithful, He is going to reward every one of us according to our work. The work you do for the Lord - the work of faith, walk, work, preach, help, pray, evangelize - all by faith. The office or post you hold in the church might not have a big name or great title attached to it, but it is a labour of love and patience of hope in which you need to be faithful, loyal, committed and selfless when discharging your duties because your work shall be rewarded. *"But watch thou in all things, endure afflictions, do the work of an evangelist, make full proof of thy ministry"* (2 Timothy 4:5).

Faithfulness in a little office brings promotion to a bigger office. If you are a faithful soulwinner today, tomorrow, God will make you a dynamic preacher or evangelist. Whatever lowly position you think you occupy today, if you would be faithful, higher positions than you would ever dream of await you tomorrow. As in the case of David (1 Samuel 16:11), you might be the youngest and unrecognized, but if you are faithful in little, God will bring you to the limelight of greater honour and service.

Remember Joshua's appointment after Moses' death and Elisha's appointment after Elijah's transition. You should however, avoid murmuring, bitterness and complaint which fill the service of some. These will block your chances of promotion to something higher and greater. Therefore, be faithful; faithfulness will earn you favour, make you admired, fruitful, spotless, remain in fellowship and promote you. "That thou keep this commandment without spot, unrebukable, until the appearing of our Lord Jesus Christ" (1 Timothy 6:14).

Rewards are just payment for anything done well; but the rewards for faithful burden bearers are timeless, eternal and of utmost benefit to men in their generations and those coming behind them. "The fruit of the righteous is a tree of life; and he that winneth souls is wise" (Proverbs 11:30). The soul winner is God's great ambassador who looks ahead to seeing a host on their way to the sunshine country. The soul winner drinks of the fountain of the water of life freely (Revelation 2:6-7). They will inherit all things and God will be their portion. The soul winner shall shine as the brightness of the firmament (Daniel 12:3). The soul winner will have the privilege of answered prayers (Matthew 7:7) and remain a conqueror in all things. The rewards are manifold and varied. I know he is going to continue to smash the head of the devil and his cohorts continually.

Above all, there are eternal rewards for the faithful servants of God among which are the following:

Incorruptible Crown (1 Corinthians 9:25-27). This is the victor's crown. It will be given to those who have exercised self-control and kept their bodies in subjection to the Lord. By the power of the Holy Spirit, these disciples restrain their appetites and lusts so as to be ready and available for ministry. Christian eunuchs and heart-wholes who are deliberately celebate for the sake of missions and the Kingdom of God fall into this category.

Crown of Rejoicing (1 Thessalonians 2:19). This is the soul winner's crown. It is meant for those who faithfully obey the Great Commission and evangelize the lost. They will receive the Crown of Rejoicing.

Crown of Righteousness (2 Timothy 4:8). This crown is for those who are watching, living ready and who love the Lord's appearing. They are the saints who eagerly await Christ's second appearing and they will receive this crown.

Crown of Life (James 1:12; Revelation 2:10). This crown is for those who suffer, endure temptation and still hold fast to their confession of faith in Jesus passing through tribulation and even death. It is **a reward for special acts of service and perseverance under trial and persecution.**

Crown of Glory (1 Peter 5:1-4). This crown is for those who lovingly serve as shepherds of Christ's flocks and faithfully teach God's word and disciple others in the faith. They will receive the elder's Crown of Glory.

As the faithful will be receiving the blessed crowns from the Lord, so also, curses and eternal punishment await false preachers. "Cursed be he that doeth the work of the LORD deceitfully, and cursed be he that keepeth back his sword from blood" (Jeremiah 48:10).

Some people will also have crowns awaiting them in Heaven for divinely-approved works done on earth but the requirement to make it to Heaven would be missing in their lives; hence, their reward goes to other stewards who are faithful to the end. "And say to Archippus (your name), take heed to the ministry which thou hast received in the Lord, that thou fulfil it" – Colossians 4:17. My sincere prayer is that we shall both make Heaven and receive our crown(s) in the mighty name of our Lord Jesus Christ, Amen!!!

E-mail prayer requests and praise reports to:
akindewum@gmail.com

REFERENCES

John R. Rice (1941). The Soul Winner's Fire. Kessinger Publishing, LLC, 2010. Whitefish, Montana United States

Leonard Ravenhill (1959). Why Revival Tarries. Bethany House Publishers.

The Holy Bible (King James) Authorized Version (1611)

Internet Resources
https://carm.org/what-is-evangelism
https://hymnary.org
https://www.gospeltruth.net>soulwinning
https://www.thegospelcoalition.org/article/105-people-die-each-minute/
http://www.thetravelingteam.org/stats
The 10/40 window. (joshuaproject.net)

CPSIA information can be obtained
at www.ICGtesting.com
Printed in the USA
BVHW031034271219
567959BV00005B/73/P